Greetings From TucsaDelphia

BY LIZ & BETH HAWKINS

Travel-Inspired Projects from Lizzie B Cre8ive

KANSAS CITY STAR QUILTS
Continuing the Tradition

Greetings from Tucsadelphia
Travel-Inspired Projects from Lizzie B Cre8ive

By Liz & Beth Hawkins of Lizzie B Cre8ive
Editor: Kent Richards
Technical Editor: Jeri Brice
Book Design: Amy Robertson
Photography: Aaron T. Leimkuehler
Illustration: Lon Eric Craven
Caricatures: Lon Eric Craven
Production Assistance: Jo Ann Groves

Lizzie B Cre8ive
Website: www.lizziebcre8ive.com
Retail shop: www.shoplizzieb.com
Email: lizziebgirls@gmail.com

Published by:
Kansas City Star Books
1729 Grand Blvd.
Kansas City, Missouri, USA 64108

Library of Congress Control Number: 2010920136

First edition, first printing
978-1-935362-33-3

Printed in the United States of America
by Walsworth Publishing Co., Marceline, MO
To order copies, call StarInfo at
(816) 234-4636 and say "Books."

contents

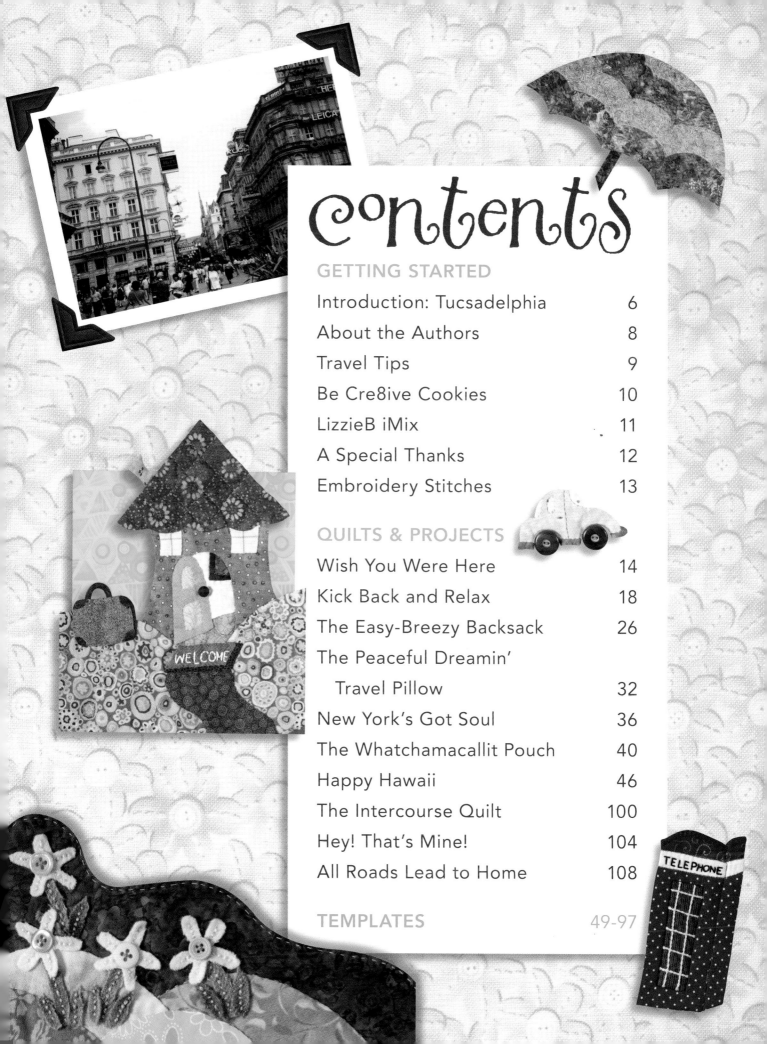

tucsadelphia

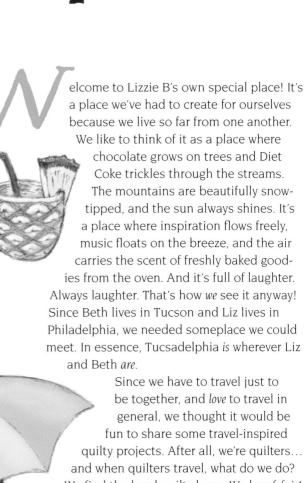

Welcome to Lizzie B's own special place! It's a place we've had to create for ourselves because we live so far from one another. We like to think of it as a place where chocolate grows on trees and Diet Coke trickles through the streams. The mountains are beautifully snow-tipped, and the sun always shines. It's a place where inspiration flows freely, music floats on the breeze, and the air carries the scent of freshly baked goodies from the oven. And it's full of laughter. Always laughter. That's how *we* see it anyway! Since Beth lives in Tucson and Liz lives in Philadelphia, we needed someplace we could meet. In essence, Tucsadelphia *is* wherever Liz and Beth *are*.

Since we have to travel just to be together, and *love* to travel in general, we thought it would be fun to share some travel-inspired quilty projects. After all, we're quilters… and when quilters travel, what do we do? We find the local quilt shops. We buy *fabric!* We gather little bits of all the places we've visited and bring them home with us. Maybe we take those bits and weave them into a quilt; like Liz's French Garden quilt. Maybe we put those pretty cuts of fabric in a basket in our sewing room, just so we can look at them and remember the place

(pronounced: TOO-sa-DEL-fee-a)

Throughout the book you'll find stamps created from sketches and watercolors by Liz Hawkins. Many of the drawings were done during Liz's great European adventure as a traveling art student. There's an enlightening story associated with these drawings on page 22, Domodossola (pronounced do'mo-dos'so-la). It's a must read.

we visited; like Beth's basket of tartan wools from Scotland. They make us smile and feel warm and fuzzy inside as memories of our travels flood back to us. We've scattered stories throughout the book of our travels together and how we've been inspired by the places we've been. We hope they jog certain memories you've had too, and give you ideas of what to do with *your* travel stash.

Join us in Tucsadelphia! Wander through the pages of our laughin' place. Enjoy a cookie or two, download our music playlist and make a quilt. Whether you're coming or going, find the time to enjoy the places you've been, look forward to the places you'll go, and be happy where you are. After all, a moment lasts all of a second, but a memory lives on forever. Go ahead. Make some memories!

peace
& love,
the lizzie b girls

we've been everywhere!

Well not quite, but we're workin' on it.

Liz Hawkins has lived in Utah, Michigan, Pennsylvania, Switzerland and France. She's traveled to Greece, Italy, Austria, Germany, Liechtenstein, Finland, Belgium, England, Ireland, Mexico, the Caribbean; Florida, North Carolina, Alabama, Georgia, Kentucky, Virginia, Maryland, Washington D.C., New Jersey, New York, Ohio, Illinois, Indiana, Wyoming, Idaho, Oregon, Washington, California, Hawaii, Nevada, Arizona and Texas. She currently resides in Berwyn, Pennsylvania, with her husband and four kids.

Beth Hawkins has lived in California, Utah, Florida, Alabama and Arizona. She's traveled to Australia, Scotland, England, Spain, Italy, France, Netherlands, Switzerland, Germany, Mexico, the Caribbean; New York, Maine, Virginia, Nevada, Massachusetts, Georgia, Mississippi, New Mexico, Pennsylvania, West Virginia, Indiana, Minnesota, Colorado, Oregon, Idaho, Washington, South Carolina, Tennessee, D.C., Maryland, New Hampshire, Hawaii, Ohio, Kentucky and Texas. She currently resides in Tucson, Arizona, with her husband and the youngest two of her four kids.

top 10 travel favorites

Lizzie B says don't leave home without...

Traveling abroad. *Above: Annecy, France. Below: Avignon, France.*

1 **A unique suitcase.** Liz's has cow spots, and Beth's has polka dots! (And don't forget to tuck the chocolate stash in there somewhere...)

2 **Music.** This is essential! We don't leave home without our iPods.

3 **A good book.** Nothin' better than sittin' on a plane or train with a good read.

4 **Travel pillow.** Planes, trains or automobiles...ya gotta keep that neck from getting stiff. (And it might as well be a **cute** one!)

5 **Warm fuzzy socks.** Great for the plane **and** questionable hotel carpet!

6 **A camera.** Gotta catch all the great smiles in all the great places.

7 **Comfy PJ's.** Maybe a couple of pairs. Preferably **cute**!

8 **Travel journal, sketchbook and of COURSE, a stitchin' project!** (OK, that's three things but we'll count them as one this time.)

9 **Duct tape.** Seriously, you never know when ya gotta fix somethin' when you're on the go! (We personally like the colorful variety...)

10 **And don't forget...clean undies!!!** (Mama says, after all...)

be cre8ive cookies

MAIN INGREDIENTS:
1 cup butter, softened
1 ½ cups brown sugar, packed
2 eggs
1 teaspoon vanilla (bourbon, of course!)
2 cups flour
1 cup oatmeal
½ teaspoon salt
1 teaspoon baking soda

In a large bowl, cream together butter and brown sugar. Add eggs and vanilla., mixing well. Add flour, salt, baking soda and all other mix-ins. Stir until well-blended. Drop by tablespoonfuls onto a non-stick cookie sheet. Bake at 400 degrees for 6 minutes.

MIX-IN'S:
1 cup chocolate chips
½ cup shredded coconut
½ cup dried cranberries
½ cup choco-covered pretzels,chopped

Be Cre8ive! Choose your own mix-in's! Use up to 2 ½ cups of any combination you like. (If you use ½ cup for each mix-in, you get to choose 5!) Try raisins, chopped nuts, trail mix, white chocolate chips, peanut butter chips, crunchy granola, yogurt covered raisins, chopped up caramel popcorn even. The sky is the limit! Everything goes with these yummy trail blazers!

iMix, you mix, we mix...

The Lizzie B girls always travel (and quilt) with an iPod!
Here's some music for the journey. (Downloadable at iTunes.
Search "Tucsadelphia" in the iMix section!)

Fly Me to the Moon, Joshua Radin
Sentimental Journey, Doris Day
Last Train to Clarksville, The Monkees
Escape, Rupert Holmes
I Love Paris, Ella Fitzgerald
New York, New York, Mel Torme
Philadelphia Freedom, Elton John
Amish Paradise, "Weird Al" Yankovic
Route 66, Marc Toussaint
I Left My Heart in San Francisco, Tony Bennett
Happy Hawaii, Abba
Sweet Home Alabama, Lynyrd Skynyrd
Always Something There To Remind Me,
   Naked Eyes

You'd Be So Nice to Come Home To, Steve Tyrell
On The Sunny Side of the Street, Keely Smith
New York State of Mind, Billy Joel
Home, Michael Bublé
Africa, Daryl Hall & John Oates
Take Me Home Country Roads, John Denver
Will You Remember Me, Rosanne Cash
Many the Miles, Sara Bareilles
Arizona, Mark Lindsay
America, Simon & Garfunkel
Every Time You Go Away, Hall & Oates
Across the Universe, Rufus Wainwright

a special thanks
to our traveling companions

ok. When we wrote our first book, we honestly didn't think we'd be writing our second one less than a year later! Now, we know it's common for authors to cut-and-paste the same old "thanks" that was printed in their previous books, especially if they are so fortunate to get the very same people on their team. But not so here at Lizzie B! You may have noticed, we like to be different. (Hence our really bizarre book titles…)

So back in late June we got an email from the folks at *The Kansas City Star* that started like this: "Okay, are you guys sitting down?" This is always an ominous sort of question. But it was followed by, "Don't panic." We took a deep breath, tried *not* to panic, and read on…they wanted us to do another book, *but* how would we feel about a February release date? Our minds quite literally went blank! So yet again, our *first* thanks must go to Doug Weaver and Diane McLendon at *The Kansas City Star* who believed that we could actually pull off such a feat, and who continually give us the room we need to be our crazy selves. Our *only* stipulation in doing the second book so quickly was that they would promise to let us have our exact same team. Our editor, Kent Richards, should really think about changing his name to Elizabeth Ann so he can be Lizzie B number 3! On second thought, don't change your name Kent, you *know* you're part of our team forever. Thanks for being there for us at all times of the day and night, and for constantly cracking us up. You *rock*! Also from the Kansas City Star lineup: Aaron Leimkuehler, Eric Craven, Jo Ann Groves, Jeri Brice and our amazingly talented book designer Amy Robertson. You are the most fabulous team *ever*! And yes…expect a big box of cookies comin' your way for all you do for us. Thank you.

Then there's our "sweat shop" in California…otherwise known as the unstoppable, most amazing quilt-whipper-upper Carole Price (lovingly called Mama C!) who unquestionably deserves the top mention when it comes to *anything* Lizzie B. She's right there ready to stitch. And when she's not stitchin', she's cracking the whip getting us into gear. Mama, we love you…you know we do! Another thanks goes to "Sister-B-Cre8ive" Christine Reyes, who continues to update our website and not only makes it beautiful, but makes it work, too! She was also the "cookie" photographer for this book. And Lauri Drean, our long-arm quilter whom we *still* have not met in person! But she made time for us and beautifully stitched our quilts once again. A special thanks to our wonderful friends in the quilty world who buoy us up and inspire us. Our fans on Facebook helped us find quotes, encouraged us when we were down, inspired us when we hit a brick wall. They are the best fans ever!

Last but never least…the biggest *thanks* goes to our husbands and our kids. They often roll their eyes at us, but deep down we know they love our creative wackiness! Thanks guys, for doing the laundry when it was stacked to the ceiling, and cooking the dinner when you found us still in our pj's at 7 p.m. working away. We love you all more than words could ever say!

And again…to God, for giving us each other. *Merci Beaucoup*!

embroidery stitches

STEM STITCH

Working from left to right, bring the needle up through fabric on the line to be stitched. Take short, uniform stitches along the traced line, while holding the loop of thread towards the left side. Bring the needle up and out of the fabric to the left at the end of each previous stitch. Keep the stitches small and uniform.

When stitching a curved line, make sure that the needle always passes the previous stitch on the inner edge of the curve. So, as a curve changes directions, you will need to "flip" your stitches too, in order to keep the stitches on the inner edges of the curves. Take smaller stitches if the curve is tight…this will create smooth curves!

BACK STITCH

Working from right to left, bring the needle up through fabric on the line to be stitched, starting on the LEFT side of the first stitch. Take short, uniform stitches along the traced line. Bring the needle up through the fabric at twice the length of a stitch. Place the needle back down on the right side, and repeat. Keep the stitches small and uniform. When stitching a curved line, take smaller stitches to create smoother curves.

Begin

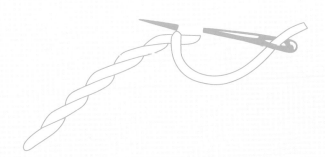

wish you were here

55" x 73"

I see London, I see France...and a whole lot of other fabulous places to visit! Let's face it, when you get a postcard that says, "Wish you were here" don't ya just want to say, "Me, too!"? Here, quilting meets scrapbooking in a whimsical way, displaying memories of places you've been to and people you've been there with. Add as many postcards or pictures as you desire! Be inspired by the places you've seen. Add fabric you've picked up along the way. Bring back the memories and share your showpiece of adventure with others!

CUTTING INSTRUCTIONS

* From each of the 5 black fabrics, cut 4 squares 9½", 4 squares 5 ½", 8 rectangles 2½" x 9½", and 8 rectangles 2½" x 5½". (You will have a total of 20 large and 20 small squares, and 40 small and 40 large rectangles.)
* From the border fabric, cut 7 strips 5½" wide x width of fabric.
* From the tan fabric, cut 13 rectangles 7" x 10½" to use for the postcards.

SEW THE BACKGROUND

1. The pieced blocks consist of a small square of one fabric, with a frame of a different fabric. Sew a pair of small rectangles to the top and bottom of the small squares, and press towards the outside. Sew a pair of large rectangles to each side of the square, and press towards the outside. Repeat to make 17 pieced blocks (you will have a few pieces leftover). Each block should measure 9½".

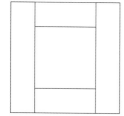

Wish You Were Here. *Postcards, memories and quilting! Made and quilted by Beth Hawkins.*

FABRIC REQUIREMENTS

■ 5 different black fabrics for background, ¾ yard each
■ Border, 1¼ yards
■ Tan for postcards, 1 yard
■ Assorted fabrics to use for appliqué, and assorted "motif" fabrics to use for stamps
■ Perle Cotton: size 5, in light tan and dark brown for postcard details
■ Two large buttons for the taxi wheels, 3 small buttons for flowers on the Russian dolls
■ A small 1" square metal buckle for the cowbell, if desired
■ A tiny buckle for the luggage tag strap, if desired
■ Medium cotton ric-rac or other cotton trim, in natural or tan, for a few of the postcard edges, 1 yard per postcard (you decide how many!)
■ Fabric printer sheets for scrapbook photos (you must have an inkjet printer and digital photo images on your computer)
■ Binding, ⅝ yard

2. To make the quilt center, use 18 solid blocks and 17 pieced blocks, alternating as you sew. Sew 5 blocks together to form a row, and make 7 rows. See diagram. The quilt center should measure 45½" x 63½".

APPLIQUÉ

1. Use your favorite method of appliqué to complete the designs on the quilt.

2. Cut out the postcard rectangles from the tan fabric. We made 13 postcards, with a finished size of 6½" x 10". Depending on which appliqué method you use, you may need to add a seam allowance to this measurement.

3. Trace a line down the center of each postcard, and also trace the lettering on each. Embroider the center lines using light tan Perle Cotton, and for the lettering, use a dark brown Perle Cotton. Stitch using a stem stitch.

4. Cut a "stamp" for the corner of each postcard. We used random fabrics, some with motifs that kind of matched the postcard theme. Vary the shapes and sizes, just like regular postage! Appliqué in place.

5. Cut out the remainder of the appliqué shapes for the blocks. Place and stitch the pieces in numerical order. We stitched as much of the appliqué as possible onto each postcard before placing onto the quilt center, to make the stitching a bit easier!

6. Scatter the postcards all over the quilt center, following the photo for placement. Stitch in place. On a few of the postcards, add some trim either underneath or around the edges for a vintage, ripply postcard look!

FABRIC PHOTOS

1. Personalize your quilt by adding your own photos… but don't be afraid to leave some room on your quilt to add more photos later, even after it is quilted. Just like a scrapbook, you can keep adding to it.
2. Select your favorite vacation photos for scrapbooking onto the quilt! You can play with photo editing software to crop, tweak colors, etc. before printing. Create a layout with word processing software, and place as many photos on one letter-sized sheet as you can. Remember to leave room for a seam allowance so you can appliqué the photos onto the quilt.
3. Print the photos onto fabric printer sheets, and be sure to follow the package directions.
4. Trim around each photo and prepare it for appliqué.
5. Make "photo corners" for each photo to add to the vintage scrapbook feel of this quilt. Cut 4 1½" squares per photo, using the tan postcard fabric.

6. Fold the squares in half diagonally, and press. Then press each raw edge under ¼" to create a photo corner.
7. Slide four corners onto each photo, and stitch all around the outside to secure to quilt. Leave the diagonal folded edge unstitched, so it looks a bit dimensional.

MAKE A QUILT LABEL

✶ Don't forget to label your quilt! Use the luggage tag template on page 53 to make a label for the **front** of your quilt. Use a small metal buckle, if you wish, on the strap. You can embroider your name and details, or use the fabric printer sheets and your computer to type your information.

ADD THE BORDERS

1. Measure your quilt top to ensure that it is 45½" x 63½". If it differs, then adjust the border lengths accordingly.
2. Join two 5½" wide border strips together, and trim to a length of 63½". Sew to the side of the quilt. Repeat to make a border for the other side.
3. Join three 5½" wide border strips together, and trim to make two borders that measure 55½" long. Sew to the top and bottom of the quilt.
4. Quilt, bind, and enjoy. Happy travels!

kick back and relax

18" x 28"

Sometimes you just need a moment. Just **one** moment to sit and relax! Take that moment, close your eyes and see yourself kicking back on a beach, book in hand, the warmth of the sun all around and the sound of the ocean nearby. One deep breath and, ahhhhh! Everything is right in the world again. This little quilt reminds us to soak up every moment and make them count!

MAKE THE BACKGROUND BLOCKS
* Mountain block: From dark blue fabric, cut a rectangle 9½" x 18½".
* Banner block: From a light blue fabric, cut a rectangle 9½" x 18½".
* Beach block: From the other light blue fabric, cut a rectangle 10½" x 18½".

MAKE THE PATCHWORK BEACH
1. From 10 different tan fabrics, cut two strips 1½" wide x 10" long.
2. Sew five different strips together, as shown. Make 4 sections.
3. Subcut each section into six 1½" strips.
4. Sew the strips together to create a piece of patchwork that is 6 squares wide x 20 squares long.

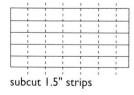

subcut 1.5" strips

FABRIC REQUIREMENTS
- Backgrounds: 1 dark blue and 2 light blues, fat quarter of each
- Tans for pieced sand: 10 fabrics, 4" x 11" strip of each
- Purples for mountains: one piece 5" x 9", two pieces 10" x 14"
- White and orange for banner, 10" x 15" piece each
- White/cream wool for clouds and flowers, 6" x 7" piece
- Green wool for leaves, 3" x 5" piece
- Small yellow/orange wool scraps for sun, 5 pieces 2" x 2" each
- Assorted scraps of fabric for remainder of appliqué
- Binding, ⅓ yard
- Perle Cotton: size 5, in black, cream, green, and to match "relax" letters
- Small black button for umbrella, 4 small yellow buttons for flowers, and 4 small black buttons for airplane
- Cording or trim for banner rope, 1 yard
- Tiny ric-rac for skirt, 4" piece

Kick Back and Relax. *Find time to enjoy the small things, and* **relax**! *Made and quilted by Carole Price.*

kick back and relax

APPLIQUÉ

* Cut out the appliqué shapes for the blocks using your favorite appliqué method. Cut the pieces for the beach (#27 and #28) from the patchwork tan fabric. Cut the wool pieces as indicated on the template, without adding an additional seam allowance. Stitch the pieces in numerical order. (The lower corner of the banner will need to be appliquéd after the quilt is assembled). The wool is stitched with matching Perle Cotton, leaving the raw edges of the wool exposed, and using a back-stitch close to the edge of each shape. Stitch the ric-rac onto the skirt piece as you appliqué.

EMBELLISHMENTS

* Embroider the quote using a stem stitch, and black Perle Cotton. Embroider the curlies at the end of the letters in "relax" according to the pattern template. Add the yellow buttons to the flower centers, and the black buttons as "windows" on the plane. Add a small black button to the top of the beach umbrella. Tack the banner rope in place, tucking the raw ends under.

PUT IT ALL TOGETHER

* Join all three panels together horizontally to finish the quilt. Complete the appliqué on the banner. Quilt, bind, and enjoy!

domodossola
(pronounced do'mo-dos'so-la)

Once upon a time, a *very* long time ago, I was a no-make-up-wearing, shave-free, mousy-haired art student backpackin' her way through Europe. Oh yes, it's true. I traded the make-up bag for a case full of watercolors, charcoal pencils, fine tipped ink pens a sketch book and loads of Arches fine art paper. And Birkenstocks. Seriously.

So. I was invited by my University to do a "Europe for the Artist" program. We started in Greece and made our way, Eurail passes in hand, west to the UK. The idea was to keep a sketchbook the entire 3 weeks, and add to that, 15 drawings and 15 paintings of whatever struck our fancy in whatever country we happened to be in. This was probably one of the *most* fun things I have ever done in my life. We channeled our favorite artists and tried to become like them. We sketched Greek temples in Greece; painted in the countryside of Germany; jumped off moving trains in Switzerland when we glimpsed a field of cows we absolutely had to paint that very minute; learned from the masters in every museum in Paris. We even stumbled upon a "secret garden" in Florence where we sat, sketchbooks and Gelato in hand, overlooking one of the most incredible cities in Europe. I became an artist in Europe. I learned to see through different eyes. I loved *every* minute! But my true adventure actually began the day my student program ended and my brother

Steve arrived. How could my experience get any more adventurous? I should probably issue a warning here. The following story could change your image of me forever! (That is, if the no make-up, hairy-legged image hasn't done so already.)

He met me in London when my study abroad was over and we had one week to travel together before my parents and other siblings came for a European vacation. By the time Steve arrived, I had pretty much blown through my savings. We sat in our little hotel room in Earl's Court, dumped our earthly belongings in a pile and assessed our situation. We had $100, my brother's first very own VISA card (a scary thing, knowing the parents aren't footing the bill anymore!), and what we referred to as our European Survival Kit. We had all that we needed, a set of watercolors, a razor blade, a pencil, English medicated toilet paper (which, honestly, looks and feels exactly like tracing paper!), and two Eurail passes; one expired with *my* name on it, and one still valid with the name Larry Pitt.

Hot gusts of air blew through our open hotel window as we sat discussing our strategy to get back to mainland Europe. We started reminiscing about our high school days and the things we got away with back then. How easily we had fooled the attendance office with our tampered absentee notices, getting multiple uses out of each by simply changing the numbers on the dates. Say you had a valid note that said you were absent on the 5th, well that 5 could turn into a 15 and even a 25. Suddenly an idea began to form. We looked at those Eurail passes. We looked at the tools we had on hand. We looked at each other and smiled! Studying the passes carefully, we noticed that in the upper right hand corner there were small boxes containing numbers for dates. The first set of boxes had the date upon which the pass became valid, the second set of boxes had the expiration date. However, the dates at that time were not computerized or typed in, no, they were *hand written*! In black ink! Well we realized that we didn't have a black ink pen, but we decided what the heck, picked up the pencil and changed the number in the month box from 06 to 07. It didn't look perfect, so we thought, what else could we do to make it look more "real"? Now Larry's pass was a two-month pass and therefore still valid. It belonged to a fellow artist who had thought he was going to stay in Europe an extra month but decided not to, giving me his pass in case my brother could use it. We noticed that on Larry's valid pass, the issuers had essentially made a mistake when issuing it in the first place. They had marked it the same dates as all the other passes in the group, but then, realizing he'd paid for an extra month, made the correction and had a little rubber stamp mark-

Europe for the Artist. *Opposite: Liz and her art traveling cronies. Above: A make-up-less younger Liz showing off her Eurail pass art. Below: Liz's brother Steve, destination Italy.*

ing near it to validate the change. I got out my handy watercolor set and the very nice English medicated toilet paper (tracing paper!) and carefully traced that nice little stamp. Next I used the razor blade to cut out the stencil of the stamp, placed it ever so gently on the newly "validated" Eurail pass, mixed just the right shade of purple and voila…had myself an extra month of travel!

We used the credit card to pay for our dinky hotel room and bid our $100 and the UK goodbye as we bought tickets to cross the English Channel. We couldn't test our passes in the UK because they have a different rail system. So our first test was going to be in France. We planned to make our way toward Dijon, southeast of Paris, where there was a family we could stay with. We got to France, found the train to Dijon and hopped on board. If we could get past these French conductors, we thought, we'd be in the clear and it would be smooth sailing (or railing!). Our Eurail passes were First Class passes, and would you believe, we actually had the chutzpah to sit in First Class?! We settled down and got comfy, keeping our eyes open for the conductor. Aside from

23

the tampered Eurail pass, we also had to worry about the possibility of being asked to show our passports with the passes to verify the names. The conductor finally got to our seats and asked for our tickets. We tried to look very natural, I held my breath and we handed ours over. It seemed like hours! He glanced at Larry's and handed it back. Then he looked at mine. He looked a little closer, shrugged, handed it back and moved on to the next seats. It worked! Sweeeet victory! We'd bucked the system yet again, only *this* time, it was the European Rail System!

From Dijon we crossed the border into Switzerland where we hopped on and off the train going from city to city. We visited Lausanne, Neuchatel, Bern, Bienne. Only once were we asked for our passports, by a Swiss conductor no less. In very smooth French Steve told him that he'd lost his passport which was why we were heading to Geneva, the only city in Switzerland with a US Consul! Oh, we were smart, weren't we? Or just freakin' lucky?? In fact, we were feeling *so* lucky we decided to take our chances one step further and cross another border into Italy. We booked a night train to Florence, making a reservation for a couchette, the sleeping car. As the conductor made his way toward us, we no longer even felt a ripple of nerves. We just handed those puppies over as we continued our conversation. However, we'd forgotten that they take your passes AND passports when you're on an overnight train. Yikes! A new set of nerves kicked in. What if they compared the passes and passports and found that Larry didn't have a passport and Steve didn't have a Eurail pass? I can't say I slept too well that night. Rubbing our tired eyes, we were awakened by sun streaming through the windows and the conductor handing back our passes and passports without saying a word. Whew! We made it again! Yes, we were high on our success of having outwitted the French, Swiss *and* Italians thus far. You know, there is just something about the feeling of satisfaction in getting something for free. And all your train rides through Europe? Priceless. (Quite literally!)

After the day in Florence we'd had our fill of Gelato and tourists and decided it was time to head back to Geneva. We sat back and enjoyed our last ride. The mountain air was so clear and the towns seemed sleepy and dreamlike. The train stopped momentarily at each town along the way. I had just enough time to write down names of some of these places vowing I'd come back to live there someday. As we pulled into the last station before the Swiss border, I wrote down the name of the town, *Domodossola*.

The train stopped, and at this point, half the train was to go back the way it came and the other half would move on to Switzerland. This meant that Swiss conductors would get on the train and ask for our passes for the last time. The conductor finally got to our compartment and we handed over the passes once again. But *this* conductor actually *looked* at the passes quite closely! He asked my brother a question in French, "It seems odd," he said, "that two mistakes like this would be found together. Where did you get these passes?" He asked for our passports. What were we to do? We handed them both over and he left. I thought I was going to *die*! We'd been caught! There was *no way* they wouldn't notice that the passports and passes didn't match up. We braced ourselves for the worst and had *no* idea how we were going to talk our way out of this one. In a foreign language? In a foreign country?

The conductor came back…with two policemen. Yep, you guessed it, they handcuffed and escorted us off the train into the police station at the border. They informed my brother that we would need to pay a fine of five hundred dollars cash or spend five days in jail and that, frankly, that was letting us off easy. Tears streamed down my face as my brother translated what was being said. We didn't have $500. Which meant not only had our luck run seriously amuck, but that we'd be spending the next five days in this rotten place! Domodossola. The thought was so terrifying. My wrists began to itch as they walked us down the musky corridor to our new home for the next few days. The sound of the shutting cell door rang in our ears as it clanged to a close and the lock tumbled into place. They let us keep our bags since there was hardly a thing in them anyway. We sat speechless and horrified, hugging our bags on the cold concrete floor. Suddenly another reality hit…we were supposed to meet our parents in Geneva in less than twenty-four hours! But *how*?

After we'd been sitting in the dusky cell for awhile, one of the officers came to check on us. It turned out he was extremely curious as to how we'd tampered with our passes. My brother then started explaining what we'd done in that

Europe for the Artist. *On a quest to paint picturesque Swiss cows dotting the beautiful countryside.*

little hotel room in London. The officer wanted to know all the places we had traveled on our passes. Uh-oh! Steve started listing the places and the near run-in's we'd had with other authorities. Then I saw it: I could have sworn it was a twinkle in his eye! (The Swiss don't give much away.) He said he thought it rather funny that we'd got by all the other authorities but finally got caught by the Swiss. He asked if he could look at our "European Survival Kit," so we showed him all our tools (I think he especially liked the English medicated toilet paper). Then he asked if I would permit him to look at my artwork. As if I was in any position to say no! He asked us why we were heading toward Geneva. We told him about our parents and the rest of the family coming over to meet us for a family vacation. When we finished, he nodded and told us he'd be back in a bit. When he returned, he had a set of keys! He told us that there was a train to Geneva leaving in 10 minutes. It was the last train of the evening and would get us there at midnight. He unlocked the door, and motioned for us to leave. Was he serious? We were stunned! Finally, the officer permitted us a full smile and said they were all amused by our story. He said his chief was still chuckling. He handed back our passes with a VOID stamped over them

and advised us not to try such a thing again, at least in Switzerland. My brother told them we had no money for the train, but they said not to worry, and gave us a pass for the rest of our journey. I reached in my bag and pulled out a painting I'd done of the Swiss city Lucerne, which I'd seen him admire. Steve asked if he would accept it as a token of our gratitude. It wasn't much, but it was at least something! He said he would be honored, smiled, and shook my hand. He then ushered us to our train and waved farewell after we found our seats. A flood of relief washed over us knowing we'd be in Geneva in time to meet our parents' flight. When we arrived, it was after midnight and we couldn't find a place to sleep. We ended up on the cold marble floor of the Cornavin train station in the center of town along with a bunch of other backpackers and European travelers. Little did I know that merely a year later, the city of Geneva would become my home and I'd pass by that spot on the floor a million times reminding me of our grand adventure. I felt the hard case of my watercolor box inside my bag, looked at my brother and smiled. The European Survival Kit! All we needed was a set of watercolors, a razor blade, a pencil and English medicated toilet paper. —*Liz*

The Easy-Breezy Backsack.
The perfect lightweight travel bag! Made by Beth Hawkins.

the easy-breezy backsack

14" x 16" x 2"

Let's face it, a back pack is a **must** when you're on the go! You need your hands free so you can snap pictures as you take in the wonderful sights. This backpack comes together easy-peasy with plenty of pocket space inside for all your travel needs. Use your favorite fabrics to make it your own...lightweight cotton, something quilted, or even laminated cloth! You'll be the envy of all your travel mates.

CUTTING INSTRUCTIONS

* From three different fabrics, cut 3 rectangles that measure 15" x 30" (one for the outside of the backsack, one for the lining, and one for inside pockets)
* Cut lightweight batting and muslin backing about 18" x 50", if quilting your backsack
* Cut one rectangle that measures 9" wide x 14" high (for the outside pocket)
* Cut one rectangle that measures 7½" wide x 6" high (for the outside pocket flap)
* Cut twelve 1" wide grosgrain ribbon lengths 3" long each, for the drawstring loops
* For fabric straps, cut four strips that measure 2½" wide x approximately 40" long, **or**...
* For ribbon straps, cut 2 lengths of 1" wide grosgrain ribbon that measure 70" long

QUILTING (optional!)

1. Quilt your fabric pieces, if you wish, before constructing the backsack. It is equally cute and functional if you choose **not** to quilt the fabric. Without batting, it is a little more lightweight, and is great for packing and travel!
2. To quilt the fabric, layer the outside lining, outer pocket, and pocket flap with the batting and muslin backing, and quilt as desired. When done, trim the batting and backing to match the edges of the pieces.

FABRIC REQUIREMENTS

▤ Outside of backsack, ½ yard
▤ Lining & outside pocket, ½ yard
▤ Inside pockets & outside pocket flap, ½ yard
▤ Straps, ⅓ yard of fabric, **or** 4 yards of 1" wide grosgrain ribbon
▤ Ribbon for loops, 1" wide grosgrain, 1 yard
▤ Velcro, about ⅝" wide, sew-on, 7" long
▤ Decorative button, if desired

If quilting your backsack, you will also need:
▤ Lightweight batting scrap, 18" x 50"
▤ Muslin or scrap backing, ¾ yard (or 18" x 50")

the easy-breezy backsack

SEWING THE LINING

1. Make the inner pockets by folding the 15" x 30" pocket fabric in half lengthwise, so that it measures 7½" x 30", and press along the fold.

2. Pin the pocket to the bottom edge of the lining fabric. Stitch the "pocket sections," by stitching straight lines from the top of the pocket to the bottom, backstitching at the top for durability. We stitched several sections in varying sizes, as indicated on the diagram, but you can tailor yours to your own needs!

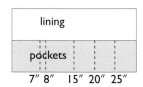

3. Fold the entire lining unit in half, pocket-side together, to form a tube. One side of the lining will be the fold, and the other will be stitched. Use a ½" seam on the side, and be sure to catch the edges of the inside pocket in the seam as you sew.

4. Partially stitch the bottom seam of the lining, using a ¼" seam, leaving a 6" opening in the center of the bottom seam, so you can turn it later.

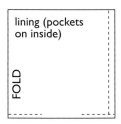

5. To make "boxy" bottom corners, fold the corners so that the side seam (or fold) matches with the bottom seam (or fold), right sides together, to form a triangle.

6. Stitch a line across the corner, that measures about 2" in length, as shown. Backstitch the seam.

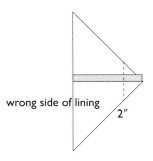

MAKE THE OUTER POCKET

1. Fold the pocket fabric in half, right sides together, to measure 9" x 7", and press.

2. Fold the flap fabric in half, right sides together, to measure 7½" x 3", and press.

3. For both pieces, stitch all three sides, using a ¼" seam, leaving a 4" opening on the long edges. Turn right side out, and press. You will close the seams up later as you sew.

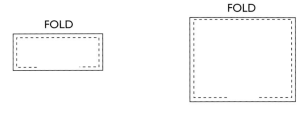

4. Topstitch the folded edge of the pocket. Trim both sides of the Velcro to 6½". Pin the loop (soft) side of the Velcro to the center top and front of the pocket edge. Sew around all four sides of the Velcro.

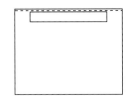

5. Pin the hook side of the Velcro to the center edge of the inside of the flap. Sew around all four sides of the Velcro.

6. To make the pocket dimensional, fold the bottom corner, as shown, and stitch ½" in from the corner point. Backstitch the seam. Repeat for the other corner.

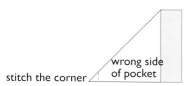

stitch the corner   wrong side of pocket

SEWING THE OUTSIDE

1. Fold the backsack outer fabric in half so that it measures 15" x 15", and press the fold line. The fold will be the **bottom** of your bag. (If your fabric is directional, just cut it into two 15" x 15" pieces, and re-sew a bottom seam so the fabric will be facing the correct way. Sew the seam again for added strength. The seam allowance of ¼" won't matter when the backsack is sewn together).

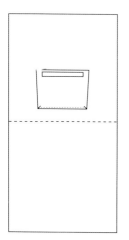

2. Place the outer pocket in the center of the backsack, about 2" up from the bottom edge. Pin and stitch **just** the bottom edge of the pocket, stitching close to the edge, backstitching at each corner.

3. Pin the sides of the pocket in place. Use a ruler to make sure the sides of the pocket are lined up straight. The pocket will be "pouchy" when pinned in place. **Don't sew it yet!**

4. Tuck the pocket flap in about ½", just behind the top of the pocket. Make sure the Velcro lines up when the flap is folded over to close up the pocket. Pin in place.

5. Now unpin the pocket back just a little, so you can get in there and stitch the flap to the bag. Stitch close to the edge, and then stitch again ¼" away from first stitching.

6. Re-pin the pocket back into place, and stitch both sides, close to the pocket edge. Backstitch at the top corners, and end at each bottom corner.

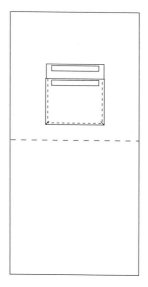

7. Sew a decorative button to the pocket flap, if you wish.

the easy-breezy backsack

8. Measure up 1½" on each side of the bag, from the bottom fold, and pin a ribbon loop (one 3" piece of ribbon, folded in half, wrong sides together), matching raw edges, as shown. (The loops will stick out on the bottom outside of the finished bag, when it is turned right-side-out).

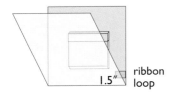

1.5"   ribbon loop

9. Pin and sew up each side of the bag, right sides together, using a ¼" side seam. Backstitch over the loops.

10. Make "boxy" bottom corners, just as you did with the lining. Fold the corners so that the side seam matches with the bottom seam (or fold), right sides together, to form a triangle. Stitch a line across the corner, that measures about 2", and backstitch.

PUTTING IT ALL TOGETHER

1. With the bag inside-out, pin the top ribbon loops to the RIGHT side of the bag. Fold each 3" ribbon in half, and pin around the top edge of the bag, raw edges together. Use 10 loops, placing one directly on each side seam, and spacing the others about 2" apart.

2. Place the lining inside the bag, matching the top raw edges, right sides together. The ribbon loops should be between the bag and the lining. (You may need to adjust the width of the lining, by graduating the seam a bit, to make it fit). Pin and sew around the top edge of the bag, using a ¼" seam. Sew this seam twice for extra durability.

3. Turn the bag right side out, using the opening that you left in the bottom of the lining.

4. Stitch the opening in the bottom of the lining closed, either by machine or by hand.

5. Topstitch around the top edge of the bag, about ⅛" from the top seam line. Keep the seam line on the top lined up straight as you stitch. This will keep your bag & lining in place, and reinforce the loops.

STRAPS

1. If making fabric straps, join two fabric strips together and trim to 70" long. Make two straps. If using wide ribbon for the straps, cut two lengths that are 70" long, and skip to step 4.

2. Fold each long raw edge in ¼" and press. (Using spray starch as you press will make this much easier!) Fold ONE short end of the strip in ¼" and press.

3. Fold each strap in half, lengthwise, wrong sides together and matching folded edges. Topstitch each strip, stitching ⅛" from each long edge. Leave both ends unstitched (one will be folded under, and the other one will have raw edges).

4. Thread the straps through the ribbon loops, in opposite directions. Start at a side-seam loop, and go around all 10 loops before going through the loop at the bottom. Tuck the raw edge of the strap into the folded edge to join the strap into one continuous piece. Stitch the strap ends together.

5. Repeat for the other strap, starting on the other side and going the opposite direction. The straps will form a drawstring and when pulled from opposite sides, will cinch your backsack closed!

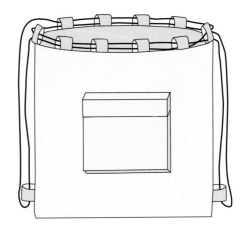

The Easy-Breezy Backsack. *Try it quilted, unquilted…*
use canvas or laminated cotton as pictured here! Made by Beth
Hawkins. Laminated cotton provided by Michael Miller Fabrics.

The Peaceful Dreamin' Travel Pillow. *Cute little appliqué pillows to accompany you on* ***all*** *your travels! Covers made by Beth Hawkins.*
Note from the editor: *When sleeping on the plane, try not to drool on the appliqué side!*

the peaceful dreamin' travel pillow
12" x 16"

How many times do you step on a plane scanning the nooks and crannies to find the **one** last remaining pillow? Because even if those darn airline pillows are scary, scratchy and barely comfortable…they're better than nothing! Well kiss those pillow-scavenger-hunts good-bye. You'll be the envy of the entire plane with a cute pillowcase on your own travel pillow. From here on out, it's happy trails and peaceful dreamin'!

CUTTING INSTRUCTIONS
* For the pillow front, cut a rectangle 12½" x 16½".
* For the pillow back, cut two rectangles 12½" x 19".

APPLIQUÉ
1. Prepare the appliqué shapes for the pillow using your favorite appliqué method. Stitch the pieces to the pillow front in numerical order.
2. Embroider the curlicue and handle on the Vespa, and the peace sign on the bus, using a stem stitch and Perle Cotton.

MAKE THE PILLOW
1. Press the backing rectangles in half, wrong sides together, so that they each measure 12½" x 9½".
2. Place one of the rectangles to the right side of the pillow front, matching raw edges towards one side. The fold of the backing fabric will be towards the center. Pin along the raw edges.
3. Place the other rectangle also on the right side of the pillow front, towards the **other** side, so that the folded edge is also near the center and is overlapping the first backing rectangle. Pin
4. Sew along the raw edges, around the entire pillow rectangle. Turn right side out, and pop in the pillow form!

FABRIC REQUIREMENTS
- Fabric for the pillow and back, 1 yard
- Assorted scraps for the appliqué pieces
- Pillow form in travel size, 12" x 16" (if using another size, adjust measurements accordingly)
- We used a really soft, down-like pillow from Bed Bath & Beyond…super comfy!

new york city's got soul

I "heart" New York! There is just something about the big city. Bright lights, crowded sidewalks, bumper to bumper traffic dotted with yellow taxis leaning on their horns. It is a city that never sleeps, that's for sure! Having grown up in Philadelphia, New York City was only a train or car ride away. I had spent winters peering through the department store windows full of the wonders of Christmas, with the scent of warm roasted chestnuts wafting through the air. Had witnessed the lighting of the tree at Rockefeller Center and ice skated beneath its glory. Spring and summer, I walked the winding trails of Central Park and hoofed it through every art museum the city had to offer as an art student in high school. But Beth grew up in California, and never having visited New York City, she decided one cold January to make the trip for the first time. We planned to hit the fabric district and visit with Henry Glass Fabrics, our soon-to-be partner in the fabric industry.

Now, in retrospect, I'm not sure why we chose January for a girl coming from Arizona to make her first trip to New York! She had to buy a wool *coat* for one

thing. And dig out the scarf, hat, gloves…etc. Beth flew into Pennsylvania first, so that we could do an event at my local quilt shop. It isn't often we get to do this together, and it's *always* a lot more fun together! After the workshop, we hopped on the train and made our way to the Big Apple. We booked ourselves a hotel room right on Times Square. Beth wanted the *whole* experience! The first thing she noticed was that it looked like high noon in Times Square even at midnight, the lights were so bright. We had such a fabulous time together. I got to introduce Beth to a real New York deli and *real* New York cheesecake (which we pretty much ate for dinner every night. Just the cheesecake that is…). We went to the Half Price Ticket booth and caught a Broadway show of Mamma Mia. And we were like two kids in a candy shop in the fabric district, especially in the notion shops! Buttons, ribbon and trim, oh my!

Beth enjoyed her New York experience *so* much in fact, that she decided to bring her family back in the summertime to see it too. They ventured back in June this time, Beth, her

hubby, kids and even her parents, Bob and Carole (Mama C!). My family went up to spend a day with them, and wouldn't you know it, we chose to visit NYC during Gay Pride weekend! The day we got there was the day of the big parade. Walking to Central Park was a site we'd never forget. Rainbow boas, flags, high heels and Streisand look-a-likes. The float for the "Nair" men was a sight to behold. Oh yes, who wears short-shorts? We walked and walked through the city that day since it was a gorgeous day, and all the streets were blocked off for the parade anyway. By mid-afternoon, our feet were dog-tired! We weren't sure we'd make it back to the little apartment Beth's family had rented for the week. But being New York, we soon came across a shoe store and decided instantly, we should all buy a pair of flip-flops for the rest of the journey. When Beth and I are together, it doesn't take us long to find cute shoes that we *both* love. As we made our separate ways around the store, we each picked up a pair to show the other, and what do you know? They were the *same* pair in different colors! But they were so *cute*, with polka dots and comfy insoles. Of course we knew we had to have them! And by "them" I mean, we each had to have a pair in brown with pink polka dots *and* in black with white dots. And to top off the cuteness factor, we turned them over to look at the sole and found a little "lucky" penny permanently stuck on the bottom along with inspiring words like, "grace", "friend", "joy", "happiness". In that instant it happened again. We looked at that sole, looked at each other and said, "It's a quilt"!!! Sure enough…those little flip-flops from our trip to New York inspired our quilt, "New York's Got Soul". You just *never* know when inspiration is going to hit! But one thing is for certain…it always seems to hit *more* when the Lizzie B girls are together. —Liz

New York's Got Soul. *And Rhythm! Not to mention Strength, Grace, Smiles, Friendships...etc.*
All captured in this jazzy quilt! Made by Carole Price. Quilted by Lauri Drean.

new york's got soul!

50" x 50"

"I'm taking a Greyhound on the Hudson River line, I'm in a New York state of mind…" Billy Joel got that one right! There's just something about the Big Apple, a city full of heart and soul. This quilt is reminiscent of the gray city streets and bright city lights in the city that never sleeps.

CUTTING INSTRUCTIONS

* From the assorted black fabrics, cut an assortment of 68 squares 4⅞". Label as A.
* From the additional black piece, cut 4 rectangles that measure 4½" x 8½". Label as D. Also cut 4 squares that measure 4½", and label as E. Also cut 6 squares that measure 4⅞", and label as F.
* From the dark gray fabric, cut 6 squares 4⅞". Label as B.
* From the light gray fabric, cut 8 squares 4⅞". Label as C.
* From the inner border fabric, cut 2 strips that measure 1½" x 40 ½", and 2 strips that measure 1½" x 42½".
* From the outer border fabric, cut 5 strips that measure 4½" x width of fabric.

MAKE THE TRIANGLE BLOCKS

Completed blocks will measure 4½" (to finish at 4")

1. Use 60 of the "A" squares. Mix them up to create an assortment of blacks in the blocks.
2. Place two squares right sides together, lining up the corners. Draw a line from corner-to-corner. Stitch on each side of the line, a scant ¼" away. See diagram. Cut on the drawn line to make two units. Press open. Make a total of 60 "A/A" blocks.

FABRIC REQUIREMENTS

* Assorted blacks: 9 fabrics, ⅛ yard each
* Additional black fabric, ½ yard
* Dark gray, ⅛ yard
* Light gray, ⅛ yard
* 2 greens for scrolls and leaves, ¼ yard each
* Scraps of bright fabrics for flowers, hearts, & letters
* Inner border, ¼ yard
* Outer border, ¾ yard
* Binding, ⅜ yard
* Perle Cotton: size 5, in green, and other colors matching appliquéd letters

new york's got soul!

3. Use 8 remaining "A" squares, and the 8 "C" squares. Follow the above directions for making half-square triangle blocks. Make a total of 16 "A/C" blocks.

4. Use 6 "F" squares, and 6 "B" squares. Follow the above directions for making half-square triangle blocks. Make a total of 12 "F/B" blocks.

ASSEMBLE THE QUILT

1. Make the corner blocks by sewing 3 "A/A" blocks together to make a row, as shown. Make sure the diagonal seams are all going the same direction. Make 12 rows.

2. Sew 3 rows together to make a corner block. Make sure the diagonal seams are going the same direction. Repeat to make 4 corner blocks.

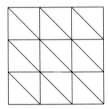

3. Make the outside-center blocks by sewing 4 "A/A" blocks together to make Row 1, as shown. Make sure the diagonal seams are placed as shown in the diagram. Make 4 units of Row 1.

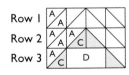

4. Sew 2 "A/A" blocks and 2 "A/C" blocks together to make Row 2. Make sure the diagonal seams are placed as shown in the diagram. Make 4 units of Row 2.

5. Sew 2 "A/C" blocks to the ends of a "D" rectangle to make Row 3. Make 4 units of Row 3.

6. Sew the 3 rows together to make the outside-center block. Make 4 outside-center blocks.

7. Make the center block by sewing 2 "E" squares and 2 "F/B" blocks together to make Row 1, as shown. Make 2 units.

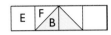

8. Sew 4 "F/B" blocks together to make Row 2. Place as shown in the diagram. Repeat to make 2 units.

9. Sew the 4 rows together, as shown. Flip the bottom 2 rows over as you sew the block to form the diamond pattern.

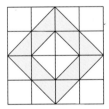

SOME O' THE APPLIQUÉ

Appliqué all of the motifs using your favorite method of appliqué.

1. Cut out 1 large heart and 4 small hearts. Cut out 4 small scrolls from the green fabric. Appliqué to the center block, using the quilt layout on page 39 for motif placement. Embroider the ends of the scrolls with matching green Perle Cotton using a stem stitch.

2. Cut out 4 sets of flowers & leaves and appliqué to the "D" rectangle in the outside-center blocks.

ASSEMBLE THE QUILT CENTER

* Sew all of the large block units together to form the quilt center. Sew in horizontal rows first, then all three rows together. Rotate the corner blocks so that the diagonal seams are oriented the right way. Use the layout guide for placement. The quilt center should measure 40½" square.

MORE APPLIQUÉ

1. Cut out 4 large scrolls from the green fabric and appliqué using the layout as a guide. Embroider the ends of the scrolls with green Perle Cotton.
2. Cut out the various letters to be appliquéd, and place according to the layout.
3. Use a marking pencil to trace the remainder of the lettering, and embroider using matching Perle Cotton.

ADD THE BORDERS

1. Measure your quilt top to ensure that it is a 40½" square. If it differs, then adjust the border lengths accordingly.
2. Sew the 1½" x 40½" inner border strips to the sides of the quilt.
3. Sew the 1½" x 42½" inner border strips to the top and bottom of the quilt.

4. Trim two of the 4½" wide outer border strips to 42½" long and sew to the sides of the quilt.
5. Join the remaining three 4½" wide together lengthwise, and trim to make two borders that measure 50½" long. Sew to the top and bottom of the quilt.

FINISH THE QUILT

1. Cut out four sets of corner flowers and leaves, and appliqué to the corners of the quilt, using the layout guide for placement.
2. Quilt and bind as desired.

The Watchamacallit Pouch.
A handy pouch for all your travel needs! Made by Beth Hawkins.

the whatchamacallit pouch

10" wide

A practical pouch for all the thingamajigs, doohickeys, whatsits, gizmos and gadgets we need when we travel! The frames come in enough sizes for you to let your creativity run wild as you imagine all the uses for this functional pouch. Cosmetics, on-the-road stitching supplies, travel chargers, even your chocolate stash! The possibilities are as endless as the long and winding road.

CUTTING INSTRUCTIONS

* From the outside fabric, cut a rectangle 10½" x 16". **If** the fabric is directional, cut two pieces 10½" x 8¼", and seam them together to make a 10½" x 16" piece.
* From the inside fabric, cut a rectangle 10½" x 16".
* From the top casing fabric, cut 2 strips 3" x 10½".
* Cut two pieces of ribbon that measure 2½" long.

MAKE THE POUCH

1. Hem the ends of the casing strips by folding under ¼" and pressing, then under ¼" again. Make sure that both casings measure the same length. Stitch up the ends to secure.
2. Fold the casings in half lengthwise, wrong sides together, and press.
3. Make a ribbon loop by folding in half, and sew the loop to the exact center of the casing, matching raw edges, and sewing just ⅛" in from the edge. Repeat for the other casing.

4. Quilt the outer fabric, if desired, using lightweight batting.

FABRIC REQUIREMENTS

■ Fabric for the outside, ⅓ yard or a fat quarter
■ Fabric for the inside, ⅓ yard or a fat quarter
■ Fabric for the top casing, ⅛ yard
■ Lightweight batting, if you want to quilt your pouch, 12" x 18"
■ Grosgrain ribbon, about ⅞" wide, 6" long
■ Hex frame, 10" size, available at www.ghees.com or in local craft/quilt/knit shops

the whatchamacallit pouch

5. Center the casing along one short edge of the right side of the outer fabric, with the ribbon loop sandwiched between. Stitch along the casing edge, using a ¼" seam, and backstitching over the loop. Repeat for the other side.

6. Flip the casings upward, and then fold the outer fabric in half, right sides together, matching the casings at the top. Stitch down the sides of the pouch, using a ¼" seam. Be careful not to catch the casings in the side seam as you sew. Press the bottom fold to make a creased line.

7. Fold the inside lining fabric in half, right sides together, and stitch down the sides of the lining, using a ¼" seam. Press the raw top edge of the lining under ¼", wrong sides together. Press the bottom fold to make a creased line.

8. To make a flat bottom for the pouch, open up one corner of the outside fabric (it's still inside out, so the right sides of the fabric are together) and fold so that the side seam matches the crease at the bottom of the pouch, to form a triangle. Pin in place. Measure 1¾" down the seam from the tip of the triangle, and draw a line **across** the seam line at that point. The drawn line should measure about 3½". Pin and draw lines for both corners of the outside pouch, and for both corners of the lining. You'll sew it all up in the next step!

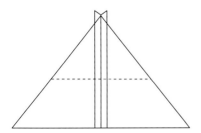

9. Place the flattened corner of the lining, seam side down onto a flat surface. Stack the outside of the bag on top of the lining, matching the flattened corners, with the seam facing up. Sew across the drawn line of both the pouch and lining at once, and backstitch to secure. Trim away the excess corner fabric, leaving a ¼" seam allowance for the boxy corner. Repeat for the other corner.

10. Turn the pouch right side out, with the lining on the inside. Turn the top edge of the outer fabric under ¼", keeping the ribbon loop free, and pin the lining to the top edge. Topstitch all around the top edge of the pouch.

ATTACH THE FRAME

* Slide each side of the frame through the casings, and follow the instructions that came with your hex frame to secure the metal ends. (It's super easy!)

* The frames come in several sizes, so get creative! Just adjust the size of your fabric accordingly…can you just imagine all the uses? One to hold your travel chargers and cords, one for all your on-the-road stitching supplies, one for your chocolate stash…endless possibilities!

The Watchamacallit Pouch.
What are ya gonna put in yours?
Make-up? Sewing tools?
Or…the chocolate stash?!

ahhh hawaii...

doesn't the name itself just conjure up the most wonderful panoramic views of ocean, sky and beach? Even if you've never been there, we've all imagined it, or seen it in movies. The place where dreams are made. We both have Hawaii stories. Sadly, not together…

LIZ

My one and only trip to Hawaii came at the most convenient time for myself. (Although my mother-in-law may see it differently!)

At the time I was experiencing my first ever winter in Michigan. The "Mitten" state is where we moved straight from Europe. When we first arrived there, I thought, whoa, I've never see so many trucks in my life! Why does everyone drive those gas guzzling trucks, we thought smugly as we puttered around in our efficient, eight drink holder-boasting Toyota minivan. Then winter hit. And I mean *hit*! We lived down a little dirt road off a myriad of dirt roads. Well, you can imagine what that looks like when 3 feet of snow suddenly hits like a huge snow globe explosion. Those dirt roads become one lane, that's what happens. And the sides of the roads are ginormous banks of snow! It didn't take long for us to figure out exactly *why* everyone drove those gas-guzzling trucks…because those were the ones that could plow right through those huge banks of snow and stop on a sheet of ice without fishtailing it into a ditch. We ditched our minivan right quick and got ourselves a veritable Michigan truck, a bright orange Chevy Suburban. It was the Great Pumpkin and the new love of my life. It meant that I wasn't snowbound all winter long.

Then one day my dear hubby came home and announced that he had a business trip in Hawaii scheduled for the end of January. And I told him flat out that if he thought he was going to leave me in the Michigan snow while he went off gallivanting to the beaches of tropical Hawaii, he had another thing comin' and it'd be in the form of divorce papers! He quickly booked me a ticket and got on the phone to convince his mom, who lives in Southern California by the way, that she really wanted to come to Michigan in the middle of winter to take care of her beautiful grandchildren. He really talked up those grandchildren, boy, because the next thing we knew, I was packing a bag full of swimwear and sundresses while his mom was heading to Michigan for the first time. I gladly traded in the keys to my 'burb for my sunglasses and high-tailed it to the airport before Grandma had a chance to really notice that the drifts of snow were as high as the second story of the house!

We flew into Honolulu, and stayed on Waikiki. Poor Doug had to attend meetings for "Geeks in Paradise" (I kid you not!) while I took my fresh pineapple and papaya and spend the day sitting on the beach, soaking up the sun and the tropical breeze. Doug had the weekend off so we rented a convertible, donned our hibiscus Hawaiian shirts and drove around the island of Oahu. We stopped at a Buddhist temple tucked away in the serene mountains, drove to a Polynesian Cultural Center, and on up to the North Shore to see the massive waves crash into shore. We saw squid drying on lines, and stopped at a pineapple farm to taste the fresh pineapple. Along the way were roadside stands where we could find tropical gifts. We finished up our tour in Pearl Harbor imagining what it was like to stand in that very place when war was declared upon our country. Though I had enjoyed myself tremendously, by the end I felt a little niggling of guilt after the phone conversations we'd had with Doug's mom. Apparently, back at the old ranch in Michigan, it started snowing and never stopped! She only dared drive

the 'burb down to the end of the street for the bus and back. That's as far as the poor California girl ventured the entire week! And I don't blame her. I will, however, be immensely grateful to her for trading me a week in the snow for a week in beautiful Hawaii.

BETH

I too, have a hubby that has had to travel to Hawaii on business. And like his brother, he too knows that a trip to *that* kind of place means that he'd better be cashing in the frequent-flyer miles for a second plane ticket! Unfortunately, these brothers that we each married are in totally different lines of work, and they don't sync their schedules like they should! So although Liz and I have had the same Hawaii experiences, it has never been while we were together.

But Liz and I did enjoy the same day-trip to Oahu…even though it was at different times. A scenic drive around the island, roadside food stands, balmy beaches, a great hamburger place in Kailua, and a trip to the pineapple plantation. (I must admit…I was amazed that those things grew on bushes! I guess in 5th grade I must have missed that day.) I didn't dare try to talk that same mother-in-law to do another week with grandkids while we flew off to Hawaii — even though we live in the sunny desert. A family friend volunteered to stay with my homebound crew.

One of the things that caught my eye while in Hawaii (besides the endless beaches…ahhh!) were the traditional hawaiian appliqued quilts. I fell in love with the history and the look of the large symmetrical blocks that depict island motifs. I just h*ad* to start a project while there! Since my hubby was busy working a few days on the island of Kauai (shooting test missiles into the air or some such thing)… I GPS'd my way over to the other side of the island to visit the local quilt shop. Picked up a book on traditional Hawaiian patterns, some bright batiks, a needle, thread, and scis-

sors. I think it's the first time I'd gone on vacation without a stitchin' project. Thought I would just read and relax on the beach and *not* wanna be creative. Ah, well. Headed back to the hotel room, where an oh-so-handy iron and ironing board was awaiting, and went to work. I actually stitched a few appliquéd blocks out by the pool on that trip. Haven't picked them up since, but someday I will drag out that project and finish my first-trip-to-Hawaii quilt.

The "Happy Hawaii" quilt in this book was inspired by my second trip to the same island; same hotel, same quilt shop. It was just a couple of years later, another missile test explosion, and another drive to the quilt shop (no GPS needed) and *wow*! Even more fabulous batiks were awaiting. I just couldn't resist the colorful stacks of fabric and just knew that I had to bring them home from Hawaii. I knew that an upcoming Lizzie B project would have to be made from batiks.

Later, as hubby and I were fearlessly driving a jeep around the island, over dirt roads and lava rocks and sandy beaches (rental car!), and finding places *not* on the map… inspiration hit! A quick glimpse of a row of colorful umbrellas perched in the sand, and I knew JUST what that quilt was gonna look like, and what fabrics I would be using. What a perfect souvenir of a fabulous trip. I don't need the t-shirt that says I've been somewhere…just need to have some fabric, and a little idea. Perhaps one of these days the Lizzie B girls will find themselves under similar umbrellas, in the sand, on a beach in Hawaii *together*. We can always dream!

Happy Hawaii. *Can you smell the tropical breeze? Made by Beth Hawkins and her stash of Hawaiian batiks! Quilted by Lauri Drean.*

52" x 64"

happy.. hawaii

Imagine waves of clear blue sea crashing onto a warm sandy Hawaiian beach. Palm trees sway as clouds drift by on the mild salty-air breeze. Bright happy batik umbrellas dot the beach adding splashes of color to this tropical paradise. Ahhhh, memories of Happy Hawaii to enjoy all year round!

CUTTING INSTRUCTIONS

* From each of the 9 tan fabrics, cut 16 squares 4½". You will need 144 squares total.
* From each of the 9 blue fabrics, cut 8 squares 4½". You will use 68 squares total.
* From the border fabric, cut 7 strips 2½" x width of fabric.

SEWING INSTRUCTIONS

The background is entirely pieced with the 4½" squares. In order to curve the water along the sand, separate sections are made from the tan and blue squares, and then they are appliquéd together to get a nice curvy edge.

1. Sew the assorted tan squares together to make a grid as shown in figure A.

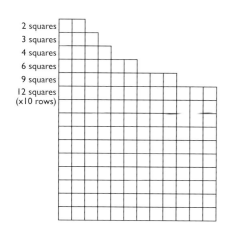

2 squares
3 squares
4 squares
6 squares
9 squares
12 squares
(x10 rows)

FABRIC REQUIREMENTS

- Assorted tans for beach: 9 fabrics, ⅓ yard each
- Assorted blues for water: 9 fabrics, ⅙ yard each
- Assorted prints for umbrellas: 18 fat quarters
- Brown for umbrella poles: one fat quarter
- Dark blue for border and binding: 1¼ yards

happy hawaii

2. Sew the assorted blue squares together to make two grids as shown in figures B and C.

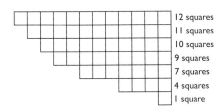

12 squares
11 squares
10 squares
9 squares
7 squares
4 squares
1 square

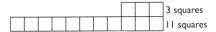

3 squares
11 squares

3. Using the layout on page 79 as a guide, draw a curved line on both of the blue grids that mimics the "water" line. Fold and press each section under along this curved line.
4. Pin the larger blue grid onto the upper corner of the tan grid, keeping the lines straight and the grid squared up. Appliqué or top-stitch in place. From the back side, trim away the excess fabric, leaving a ½" seam allowance.
5. Pin the smaller blue grid onto the lower corner of the tan grid, keeping the grid straight. Appliqué or top-stitch in place. From the backside, trim away the excess fabric, leaving a ½" seam allowance. You now have a quilt background that should measure 48½" x 60½", on which to appliqué the beach umbrellas.

APPLIQUÉ

* Use your favorite method of appliqué to complete the designs on the quilt. Stitch the umbrellas in alphabetical order, starting with the umbrella "A" in the upper corner. Each piece of each umbrella is also numbered (starting with the umbrella poles as #1) and should be stitched in numerical order.

BORDERS

1. Join three 2½" wide border strips together to make one long length. Trim to make two strips that measure 48½", and sew to the top and bottom of the quilt.
2. Join two 2½" wide border strips together and trim to a length of 64½". Sew to one side of the quilt. Repeat for the other side.
3. Quilt, bind, and enjoy the ocean breeze…!

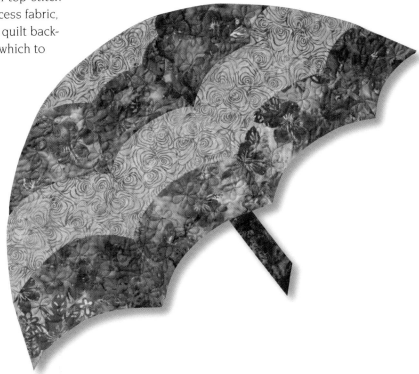

wish you were here

wish you were here

TAXI

wish you were here

wish you were here

wish you were here

wish you were here

Hawaii

London

Switzerland

Florida

Arizona

Paris

wish you were here!

wish you were here

Europe

Russia

California

New York City

Pennsylvania

Scotland

Ireland

wish you were here

6 5 4 3 2 1

9

8

7

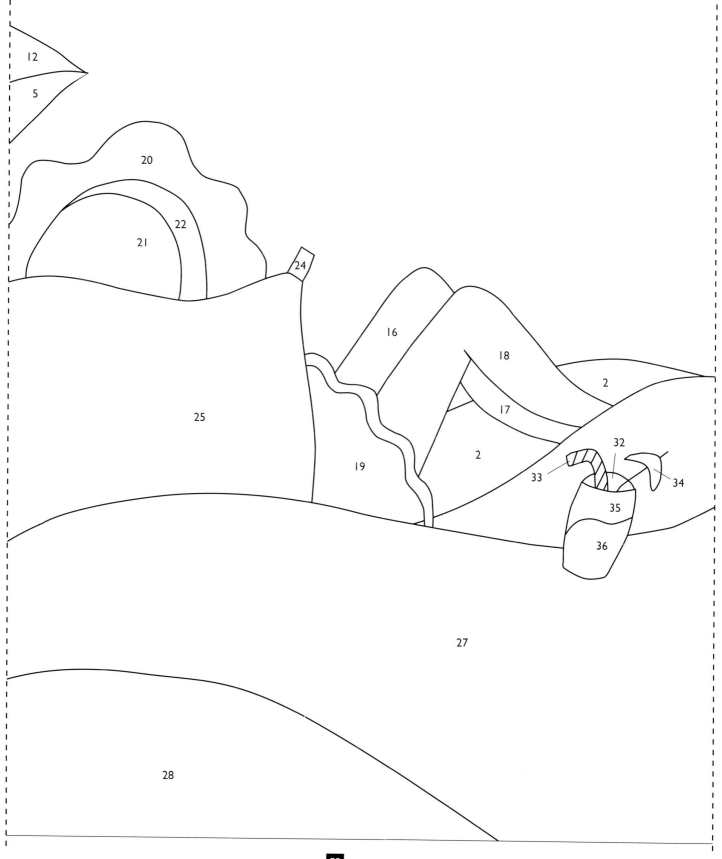

kick back and relax

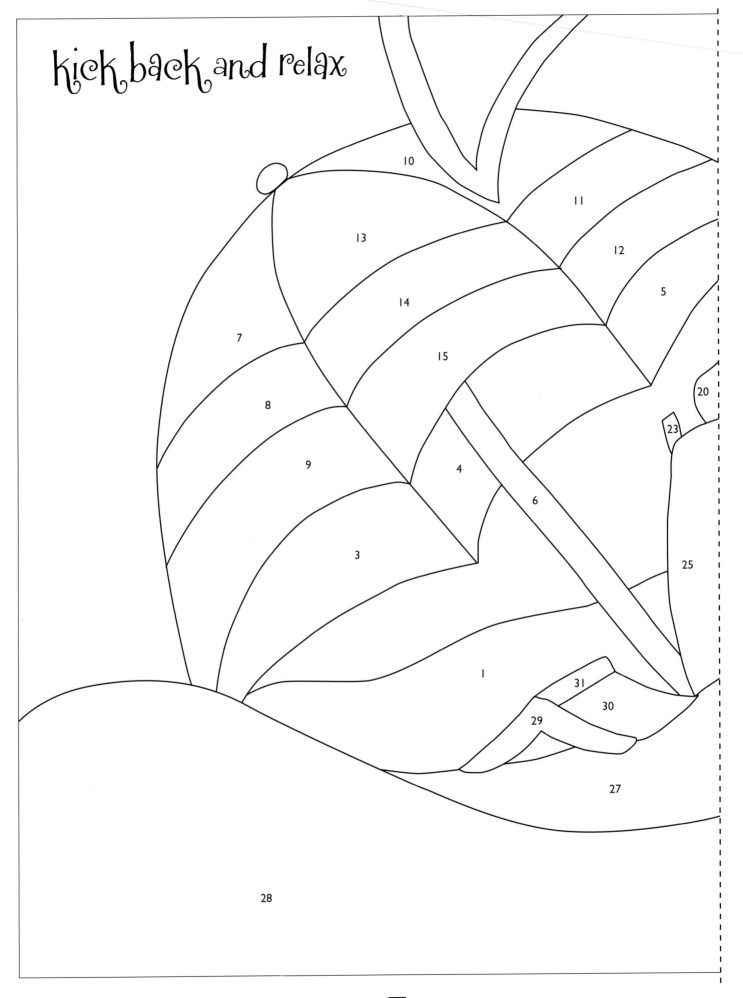

kick back and relax

26

27

kick back and relax

wool

ReLAX

Soak up e

kick back and relax

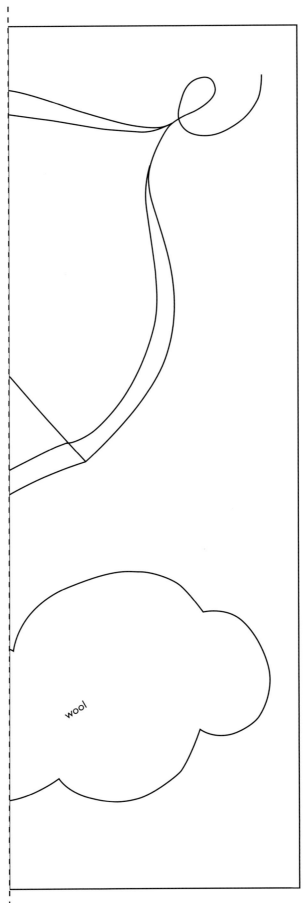

wool

WOOL
flowers and
leaves

kick back and relax

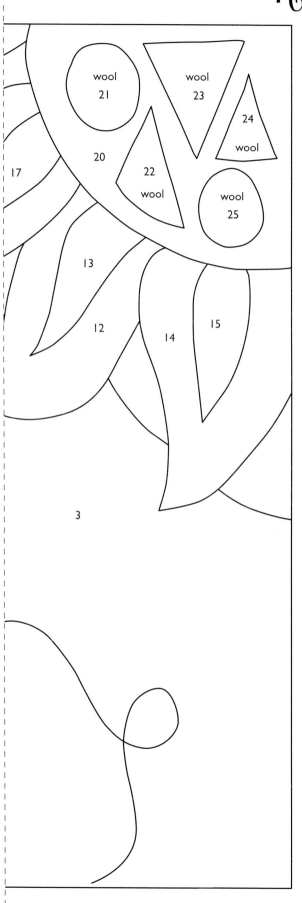

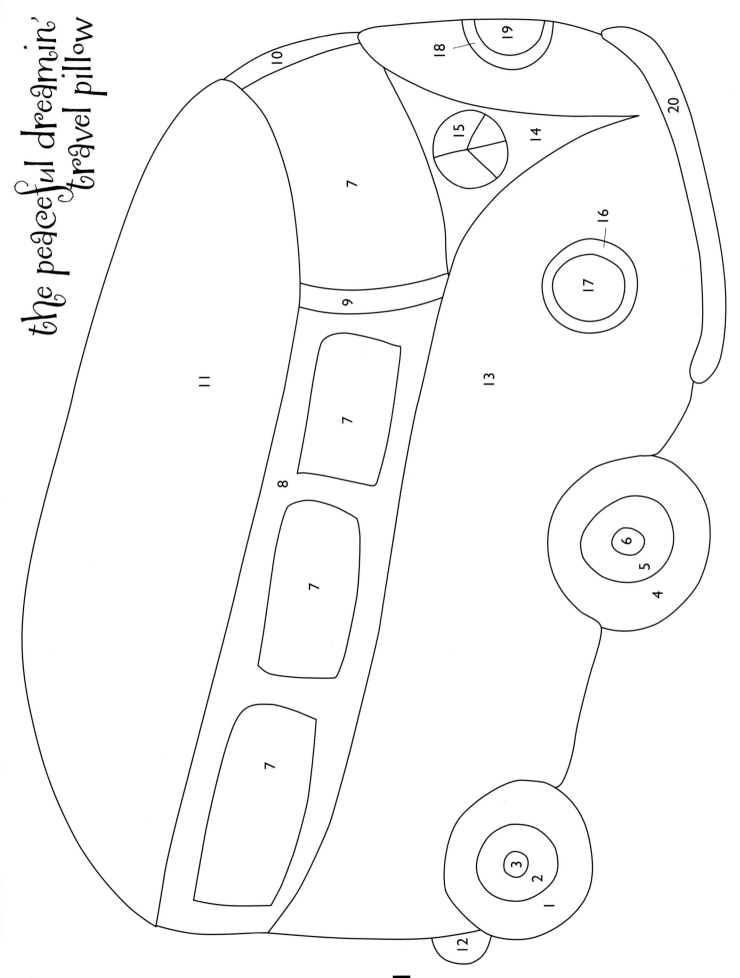

the peaceful dreamin' travel pillow

the peaceful dreamin' travel pillow

new york's got soul

Corner flower

Center block flower

1

6

5

4

3

2

large heart

small heart

small scroll

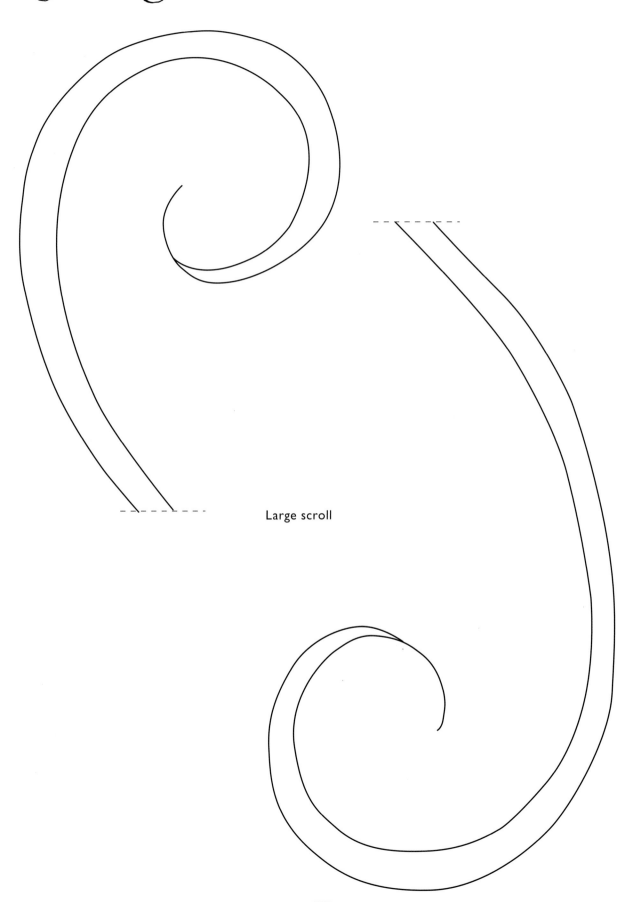

Large scroll

new york's got soul

new york's got soul

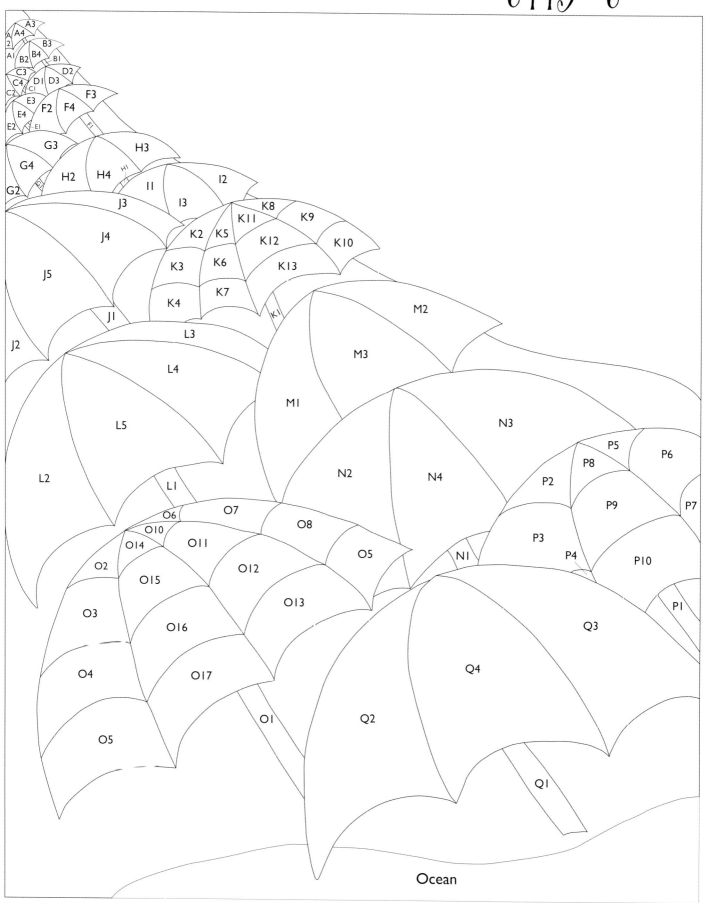

happy hawaii

A3
A4
A2
A1

B3
B4
B2
B1

C3
C4
C2
C1

D2
D3
D1

E3
E4
E3
E1

F3
F4
F2
F1

G3
G4
G2
G1

H3
H4
H2
H1

J5

J3

J4

J1

J1

I3

I1

K3

K4

connects to L3

connects to J3

connects to K2

connects to I3

K5

K7

K6

Templates are half size.
Reproduce at 200%.

happy hawaii

J2

L5

L1

O11

J1

connects to K4

L3

L2

connects to M1

Templates are half size.
Reproduce at 200%.

happy hawaii

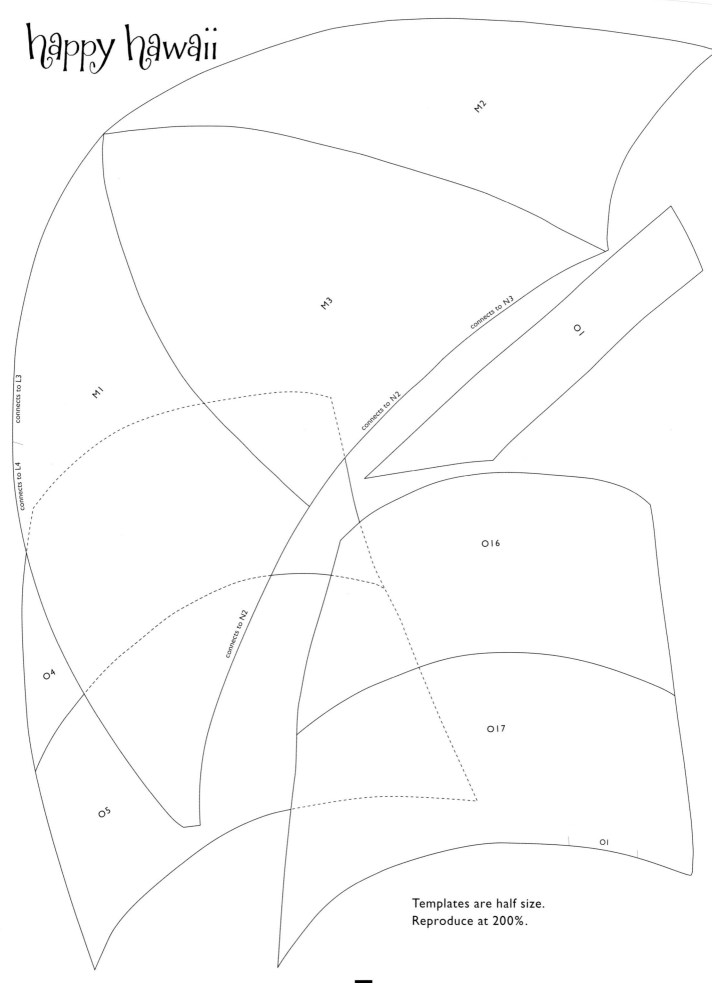

M2

M3

connects to N3

O1

connects to N2

connects to L3

connects to L4

M1

O16

connects to N2

O4

O17

O5

O1

Templates are half size.
Reproduce at 200%.

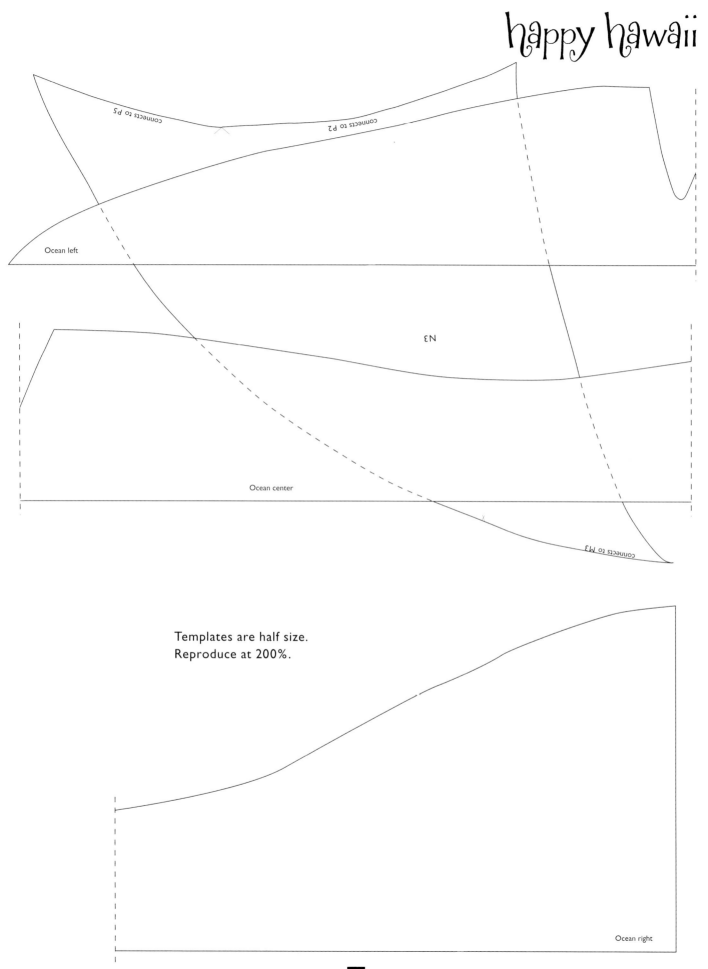

happy hawaii

connects to P5

connects to P2

Ocean left

N3

Ocean center

connects to M3

Templates are half size.
Reproduce at 200%.

Ocean right

87

hey! that's mine!

There's nothing half as pleasant as coming

all roads lead to home

again!

HOME

all roads lead to home

all roads lead to home

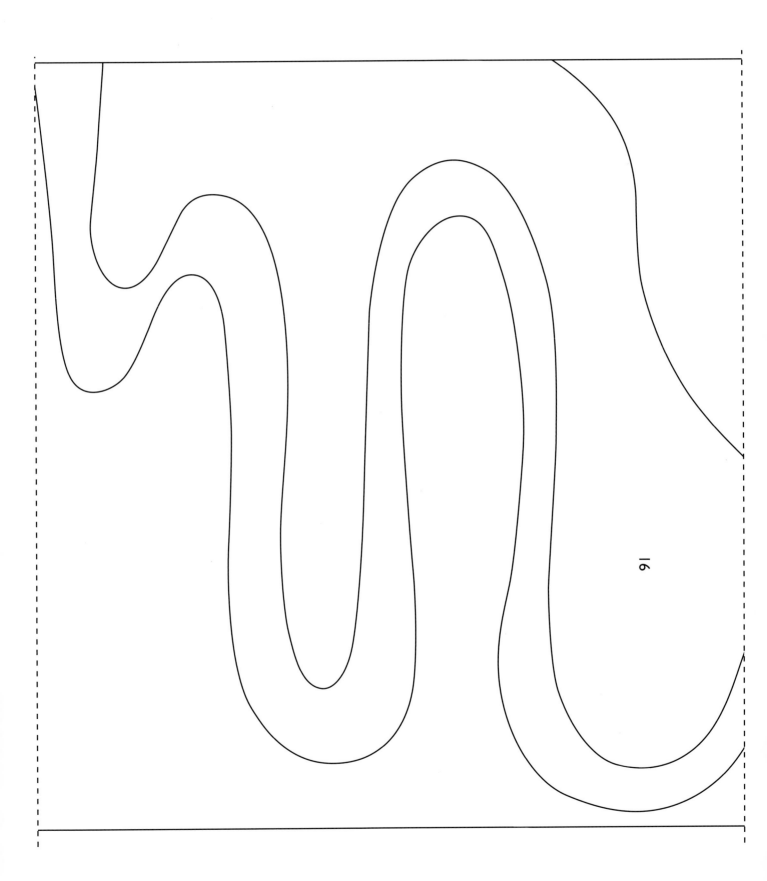

91

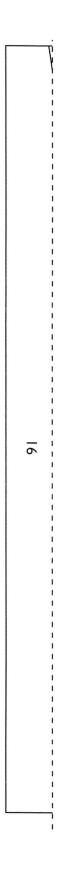

16

all roads lead to home

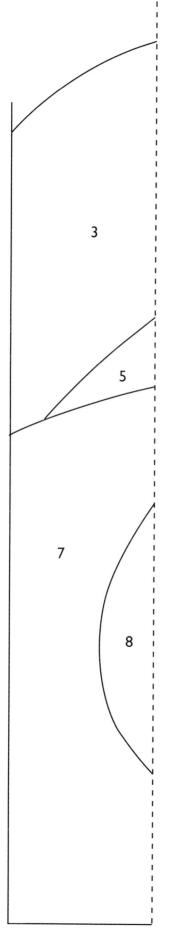

3

5

7

8

all roads
lead to home

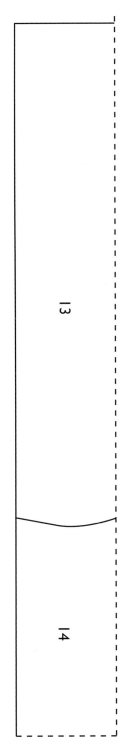

12

28
29 27
26
25

6

13

13

14

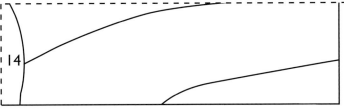

14

all roads lead to home

i love intercourse!

Well who doesn't? But perhaps I should explain as there is *no* Kama Sutra involved in this story. Maybe you'll want to read on, and maybe you won't, but here it is nonetheless. One summer a couple of years ago, I was visiting France (my old haunts for those of you who don't know me…I lived there for 10 years). My husband had meetings in the beautiful town of Evian (yes, the water really *does* come from there!) at this incredible resort up on the mountain overlooking Lake Geneva. It was *so* peaceful and serene and happened to be right after the busy school year ended so I was glad to be there and finally be able to just breathe the fresh air and recoup.

My hubby had arrived a few days before me, and being the good Lizzie B hubby that he is, he had already gone to the local Tabac (magazine store) and checked out all the French quilting magazines! (I know, he's a keeper.) He noticed an advertisement for a quilt show that was scheduled for that weekend…thinking I'd maybe want to check it out. Which, well, *duh!*

So after our few days in Evian we headed for Lyon and my first ever French quilt show. I had also seen an advertisement for a cute little quilt shop that was near Lyon, so I was hoping we could check that out too. The show itself was a

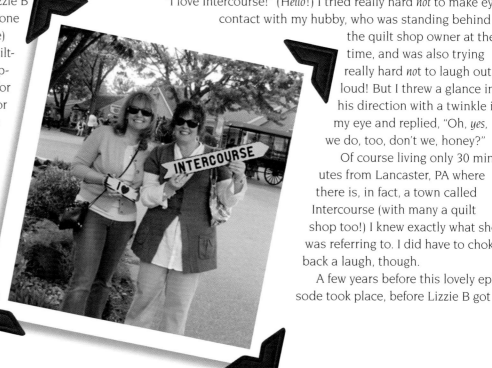

bit of a disappointment, and we were not in what you would call the "bon" part of town! In fact, it was rather scary. So we sped off to the outskirts of Lyon to find the cute little quilt shop. We drove along the winding roads through the picturesque countryside putting as much distance between us and that not-so-nice part of town as possible. When we finally found the shop I was *sooo* happy. It was darling! And the shop owner was so sweet and happy to see us. Her shop was like stepping into a local quilt store in the USA, primitive and homey with *lots* of fabric and even scented candles, and her faithful chocolate lab.

She was so excited to learn that we were from the States and asked where we lived. When I told her I was from Pennsylvania she emphatically exclaimed in clear precise English, "I love Intercourse!" (H*ello!*) I tried really hard *not* to make eye contact with my hubby, who was standing behind the quilt shop owner at the time, and was also trying really hard *not* to laugh out loud! But I threw a glance in his direction with a twinkle in my eye and replied, "Oh, *yes*, we do, too, don't we, honey?"

Of course living only 30 minutes from Lancaster, PA where there is, in fact, a town called Intercourse (with many a quilt shop too!) I knew exactly what she was referring to. I did have to choke back a laugh, though.

A few years before this lovely episode took place, before Lizzie B got

The Intercourse
Story. *Opposite above: The Royal Evian Hotel, Evian, France. Opposite below: Beth and Liz at Kitchen Kettle Village in Lancaster, PA. Intercourse or* **bust!** *Above: Our sewing loft at Deep Creek Lake, MD!*

started even, Beth came out East for a visit. We had planned a big family reunion with the entire Hawkins' clan on a lake in Maryland. But since Beth had never visited here before, she was really intent on visiting Lancaster, PA. We spent a wonderful day quilt-shop-hopping and taking in the beautiful rolling hills of green, dotted with farms. Quilts billowing in the breeze on clotheslines and over porch railings. One shop in particular had such a beautiful array of bright batiks which just happened to be on sale. What were two quilters to do? We *had* to make a quilt to remind us of our trip together. So we bought up all the bright batiks and decided to also buy some stark black, in true Amish tradition, to make the colors pop. Little did we know then, that this would be a typical Lizzie B design recipe! We didn't even know what we were going to make, but we knew we only had a week to do it while we were at the lake. It was so exciting to run home and sketch out a quickie project! We decided to make it a flip-and-stitch, quilt-as-you-go style so that we could finish it easily. The day we left for the lake, we packed up the 'burb

with my sewing machine, rotary mat and cutters, and sewing basket with all the tools of the trade.

We couldn't have asked for a better set up in the rental house. There was a little loft at the top of the stairs that was open into the family room below. We snagged a small table, moved it upstairs, found the iron and ironing board and voilà! A sewing studio for the week. Situated nicely so that we could view glimpses of the lake, and be part of the family conversations and happenings while we worked away on our keepsake quilts from Amish country. It was so fun to actually be able to work on quilts together. Up until this point, Beth and I had always worked separately, on our opposite coasts. We had a wonderful week and had a beautiful quilt to show for it. Two quilts actually, one for each of us! When they were finished, we thought we needed to name this quilt we had designed and made together, inspired by our trip to Lancaster. Well it took only but a second when we both looked at each other wide-eyed and full of mirth and exclaimed the name in unison…*Intercourse*! Of course. —Liz

The Intercourse Quilt. 37½" x 45". *Designed and made by Beth Hawkins and Liz Hawkins, July 2005.*

the intercourse quilt

37½" x 45"

Lancaster, Pennsylvania

Inspired by a visit to the little town of Intercourse in Lancaster, Pennsylvania! While this bright quilt **does** require stripping (er, fabric…) it goes together quickly with a "quilt-as-you-go" technique. Black strips frame bright batik colors stitched together to make a basket-weave effect. Nothing like a trip to Amish country for inspiration. We **love** Intercourse! PA, that is…

CUTTING INSTRUCTIONS

✳ From the green fabrics, cut a total of 72 strips 2" x 9", and 9 squares 9".

✳ From the yellow/orange fabrics, cut a total of 72 strips 2" x 9", and 9 squares 9".

✳ From the blue fabrics, cut a total of 48 strips 2" x 9", and 6 squares 9".

✳ From the pink/purple fabrics, cut a total of 48 strips 1½" x 9", and 6 squares 9".

✳ From the black fabric, cut 15 strips 1½" x width of fabric. Subcut into 60 pieces 9" long. These pieces will be used to piece the blocks.

✳ Also from the black fabric, cut 16 strips 2¼" x width of fabric. Subcut 6 strips into 24 pieces 9" long, leaving the remaining 10 strips as is. These strips will be used as the binding strips.

✳ From the batting, cut 30 squares 9".

SEWING INSTRUCTIONS

The blocks are made by layering a 9" fabric square and batting, and then sewing the strips to the top. By doing this, you will be quilting each block as you stitch. The blocks are oversized…you will be trimming the 9" squares down to 8"…so you don't need to be precise when stitching the strips.

For each block, you will use 10 strips of fabric. Two will be from the black fabric, and the remaining eight will be from the different prints. The black strips will be sewn to the outer edges of the blocks, as in the diagram.

FABRIC REQUIREMENTS

▧ Assorted green prints, 8 fat quarters

▧ Assorted yellow/orange prints, 8 fat quarters

▧ Assorted blue prints, 8 fat quarters

▧ Assorted pink/purple prints, 8 fat quarters

▧ Black for sashing and binding, 2 yards

▧ Lightweight batting: crib size, at least 45" x 60"

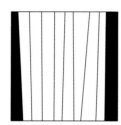

the intercourse quilt

Sew the strips onto the layered background/batting square, using a stitch-and-flip technique (described below!). It may help to use a walking foot on your machine, since you are quilting through several layers.

1. Place a batting square on top of the wrong side of a fabric square. Place a black strip even with the left edge, right side up.
2. Place a fabric strip on top of the binding strip, right sides together, and stitch about ¼" away from the right edge of the strip. You do not need to be precise, and you may vary the angles of the strips for a "wonky" look…no stress, just have fun with it!

3. Flip open the fabric strip, and finger-press it open. Place another fabric strip on top of the previous strip, and stitch. Flip open.
4. Continue until you have sewn **all** of the strips to complete the block, ending with a black strip to match the first one sewn. Remember to vary the widths of the strips, and vary the angles. It's OK if you have used only 7, or even 6 printed strips to complete the block…each one may be different.
5. Trim each block to 8". Wow! Don't those look great?

Step 1

Step 2

Step 3

Step 4

ASSEMBLE THE BLOCKS

1. Press all of the 2¼" x 9" strips and **five** of the long 2¼" strips in half lengthwise, wrong sides together.
2. Place the strippy sides of two trimmed blocks together, with the strips alternating in different directions (one vertical and one horizontal).
3. Add a folded 9" binding strip on top of the two blocks, along one edge, and matching raw edges. It will be a bit longer than the pieced block, but will be trimmed to fit later.
4. Stitch through all layers, using a ¼" seam.
5. Open up the two blocks and on the solid fabric side, pull the binding strip over the raw seam edge, so it is nice and flat, and hand stitch the folded edge down. Trim the end of binding strip to 8" to match the blocks.
6. Add more blocks to the row, until there are 5 blocks sewn together, hand stitching down the binding strip between each block. Remember to alternate the direction of the strippy piecing as you add blocks.
7. Repeat to make a total of 6 rows of blocks. Three of the rows should begin with a vertical block, and the other three rows should begin with a horizontal block.
8. Join the rows together, adding a long binding strip on top of the joined rows as you did when sewing the blocks together.
9. Open up the rows and on the solid fabric side, hand stitch the long binding strip down. Trim off the end of the binding strip to match the length of the row.
10. Repeat until all of the rows are joined together.
11. Use the remaining binding strips to bind and finish your quilt.

Hey! That's Mine! *Cute little luggage tags to set your bags apart from the crowd. Made by Beth Hawkins. Featuring Liz's kids in the Loire Valley, France.*

hey! that's mine! 4" x 5½"

You wiggle your way into the front of the baggage claim belt watching case after look-a-like case meander by while straining to find your own black bag; anxiety in the pit of the stomach that either it's lost or is taken by someone else with the exact same bag! Ease the stress of baggage claim by giving your bag a funky unique tag, easy to pick out in a sea of luggage. Next time someone reaches for **your** suitcase, this tag is all the proof you need when you say, "Hey! That's **mine**!"

CUTTING INSTRUCTIONS

* For the tag front and back, cut two pieces of fabric using the pattern template.
* For the ties, cut 2 strips 3" x 11".

APPLIQUÉ

* You can skip the appliqué step completely if you are using cute fabric…just "fussy-cut" the luggage tag shapes from the fabric to get the motif you want to show off!
* Cut out the appliqué shapes for your desired tag using your favorite appliqué method. Stitch the pieces to the tag front.
* For the Eiffel Tower design, follow the photo for placement of the trim and button.
* For the car design, add the buttons for the wheels and for the flower center.
* To appliqué a photo to the front of your tag, use word processing software on your computer to print a photo onto fabric sheets made for inkjet print ers, and be sure to follow the package directions. You can print a photo up to about 3" x 4", so that it fits onto the luggage tag. (You may want to print identification information onto the same sheet as the photo, see instructions below.) After printing, trim the photo to size, and stitch around the outside edge. Frame the photo with narrow grosgrain ribbon by sewing down the center of the ribbon and pivoting at the corners. Add a little tie at the bottom center of the photo if desired.

FABRIC REQUIREMENTS

■ Fabric for tag and ties, ⅛ yard
■ Lightweight batting, 6" x 14" piece
■ Assorted scraps for appliqué shapes
■ For Eiffel Tower: trim or ric-rac, ⅓ yard, and a button for the top
■ For the car: 2 large buttons for the wheels, and a button for the flower center
■ For a photo label, fabric printer sheets (you must have an inkjet printer and a digital photo on your computer)
■ Grosgrain ribbon for the photo label: ¼" wide, ½ yard
■ Fabric printer sheets for identification labels, or high-quality muslin and a permanent fabric marker to hand-write the labels

hey! that's mine

MAKE THE LABEL

There is room for a 3" x 4" fabric identification label to add to the back of the luggage tag!

1. Use word processing software on a computer to type the desired information, staying within a 3" x 4" section. Use fabric sheets that are made for ink-jet printers, and print according to the package directions. You may print several labels on just one sheet of fabric.
2. If you prefer, you may hand-write the labels. Use a permanent marker designed for use on fabric. Iron a scrap of freezer paper to the back of the label to make writing on the fabric easier. Remove the paper when done. Stay within the 3" x 4" size, and trim after you write.
3. Place the label onto the luggage tag back, and stitch around all four sides.

MAKE THE LUGGAGE TAG

1. Lay the tag front and back onto the batting piece, and lightly quilt all around. Trim the batting to the shape of the tags.
2. Pin the tag front and back together, right sides together, and stitch all around, leaving a 2½" opening at the top. Turn right side out, and press.
3. To make the ties, fold one strip in half lengthwise, wrong sides together. Stitch along the raw edge, leaving one end open, and curving to a point at the other end. Trim the sewn end, and turn right side out. Press. Repeat for the other tie.
4. Place about 1" of the raw ends of the ties into the opening at the top, and pin.
5. Topstitch all around the edge of the tag, about ⅛" in. Backstitch over the ties so they are secure.
6. Tie the luggage tag in a knot over a handle or loop on your travel bag. Stylish!

Hey! That's Mine! *Let your creativity run wild. There's no end to the amount of cuteness you can add to these tags!*

Please return to:
Elizabeth Hawkins
Tucsadelphia, USA
LizzieBgirls@gmail.com

All Roads Lead to Home. *There's no place like home, there's no place like home, there's no place like* **home!** *Made and quilted by Carole Price.*

all roads lead to home

18" x 28"

"Be it ever so humble, there's no place like home!" There's nothing like coming home after a long journey, no matter how near or far that journey may be. Gallivanting about on great adventures is one thing, but having a place to come back to makes it all worth it. "Mid pleasures and palaces though we may roam; home, home, sweet, sweet, home!"

MAKE THE BACKGROUND BLOCKS

* Hilly Road block: From light blue fabric, cut a rectangle 9½" x 18½".
* Home block: From black fabric, cut a rectangle 7½" x 11½".
* House block: From dark blue fabric, cut a rectangle 11½" x 11½".
* Bike Path block: From light blue fabric, cut a rectangle 8½" x 18½".

MAKE THE STRIPPY FABRICS

1. From 9 different green fabrics, cut one strip 1" wide, one strip 1¼" wide, and one strip 1½" wide, each one 15" long. (You will have 27 strips).
2. Sew the strips together randomly, varying the fabrics and widths, until you have a piece of strippy fabric that is approximately 15" x 22". Cut the appliqué sections for the hills from this piece, lining up the arrows on the pattern template with the seam lines on the pieced fabric.

APPLIQUÉ

1. Cut out the appliqué shapes for the blocks using your favorite appliqué method. Cut four leaves out of wool, as indicated on the template, without adding an additional seam allowance.
2. Stitch the pieces in numerical order. (The lower part of the bike path will need to be appliquéd after the quilt is assembled). The wool is stitched with green Perle Cotton, leaving the raw edges of the wool exposed, and using a back-stitch close to the edge of each shape.

FABRIC REQUIREMENTS

- Backgrounds, 2 light blues, 1 dark blue and 1 black, fat quarter of each
- Greens for pieced hills, 9 fabrics, ⅛ yard each
- Greens for other hills, 2 fabrics, 12" x 10" piece each
- Blue for letters, 6" x 12" piece
- Brown for bike path, 12" x 14" piece
- Small green wool scraps for leaves, 4 pieces, 2" x 3" each
- Assorted scraps of fabric for remainder of appliqué
- Binding, ⅓ yard
- Perle Cotton, size 5, in black, cream, and green
- Small button for doorknob, 2 large buttons for car wheels, one car-shaped button for the back hill
- Yellow ⅜" grosgrain ribbon for tree, ½ yard

all roads lead to home

EMBELLISHMENTS

1. Trace the details for embroidery following the photo for placement. Embroider the quote using a stem stitch, and black Perle Cotton. Embroider the lines in the road and the lettering on the welcome mat using cream Perle Cotton.
2. Add the assorted buttons, and tie the yellow ribbon around the ol' oak tree! (Cut the ribbon in half and tie a bow with both pieces, then tuck the ends under and stitch down.)

PUT IT ALL TOGETHER

*   Sew the **home** block to the top of the **house** block. Join all three panels together vertically to finish the quilt. Complete the appliqué on the bike path. Quilt, bind, and enjoy!

other star quilts books

Other Star Quilts Books by Liz and Beth Hawkins
Whimsyland: Be Cre8ive with Lizzie B by Liz & Beth Hawkins, 2009

Star Quilts Books Published in 2009
Flora Botanica: Quilts from the Spencer Museum of Art by Barbara Brackman

Making Memories: Simple Quilts from Cherished Clothing by Deb Rowden

Pots de Fleurs: A Garden of Applique Techniques by Kathy Delaney

Wedding Ring, Pickle Dish and More: Paper Piecing Curves by Carolyn McCormick

The Graceful Garden: A Jacobean Fantasy Quilt by Denise Sheehan

My Stars: Patterns from The Kansas City Star, Volume I

Opening Day: 14 Quilts Celebrating the Life and Times of Negro Leagues Baseball
      by Sonie Ruffin

St. Louis Stars: Nine Unique Quilts that Spark by Toby Lischko

Cradle to Cradle by Barbara Jones of Quilt Soup

Pick of the Seasons: Quilts to Inspire You Through the Year
      by Tammy Johnson and Avis Shirer of Joined at the Hip

Across the Pond: Projects Inspired by Quilts of the British Isles by Bettina Havig

Flags of the American Revolution by Jan Patek

Get Your Stitch on Route 66: Quilts from the Mother Road by Christina DeArmond,
      Eula Lang and Kaye Spitzli from Of One Mind

Gone to Texas: Quilts from a Pioneer Woman's Journals by Betsy Chutchian

My Stars II: Patterns from The Kansas City Star, Volume II

Nature's Offerings: Primitive Projects Inspired by the Four Seasons
      by Maggie Bonanomi

Quilts of the Golden West: Mining the History of the Gold and Silver Rush
      by Cindy Brick

Women of Influence: 12 Leaders of the Suffrage Movement
      by Sarah Maxwell and Dolores Smith